God has used Graham Power to mobilize intercession on a worldwide scale in a way few believers have ever dared to do. This is a life-changing book about one man's dreams that brought the world together in prayer. Every believer and intercessor should read it.

—Cindy Jacobs
Generals International

The Global Day of Prayer is undeniably one of the most dramatic movements of God in the past two thousand years of church history! If you sense the Lord is accelerating His work on the Earth and don't want to miss out on any of it, but be right in the middle of it, then this book is for you!

—Dr. Bruce Wilkinson, author
The Prayer of Jabez

In every century there are always a few catalytic events that impact the course of that age. There is no doubt in my mind that the phenomenon of the Global Day of Prayer will prove to be such an event for the twenty-first century. No prayer movement in history united and involved so many people and so many nations around the world to pray concertedly around the same issues. It is truly a privilege to experience, and be part of it. God always uses a man (or woman) to lead these movements. In Graham, God found a visionary person with an unwavering commitment to God's kingdom.

—Dr. Bennie Mostert
Jericho Walls International Prayer Network

In November 2000, Graham Power led me onto a balcony overlooking the Newlands Rugby Stadium in Cape Town, South Africa. As we gazed out at fifty thousand empty seats, his face lit up. "Can you see it?" he asked. "In a few months time, believers of all races will fill this place. We're going to invite God into the city!" This was Graham, the quintessential visionary. Whether he knew it at the time or not, he was prophesying the birth of what would become the Global Day of Prayer. It was an electric moment, and I am pleased that my friend has now taken the time to fill in the details of this remarkable story.

—George Otis, Jr.
Producer, *Transformations* & *FireQuest* video series

At last! A book based on a true and practical story of God's vision and work, through an obedient and willing heart who conceived it, not to store and treasure it, but to articulate it and have it birthed. Graham suffered the birth pains and experienced how God's hand worked in bringing His vision to come to pass. He never passed God's vision to someone else to carry it through, but was there himself to prove Him faithful as one who is called. To all practitioners, be encouraged and take note.

BISHOP PETER M. SEKHONYANE
FOUNDER AND DIRECTOR OF MARANATHA REVIVAL MINISTRIES
MARANATHA MISSIONS PROJECT
NATIONAL EVANGELISTIC PRAYER WATCH OUTREACH (NEPWO) AND THE
ROYAL KIDS OF SOUTH AFRICA

The testimony of Graham Power teaches that when we are obedient to God's call, great things will happen! From Cape Town to the far corners of the world, the Global Day of Prayer has become a launching pad for nation transformation. Like a mighty wave, the prayers and praise of Christians in Cape Town, South Africa, launched a spiritual tsunami that has touched nearly every nation of the world. The Global Day of Prayer, beginning with the story of one man's obedience to the call of God, will inspire you with greater faith for the transformation of nations!

—REV. DR. GREG PAGH
TRANSFORMATION CHURCH PASTOR
CHRIST CHURCH, OTSEGO, MINNESOTA

The Global Day of Prayer Movement has every characteristic of divine inspiration and surprises. First of all, it was ignited through the obedience of a lay Christian businessman. Secondly, it came out of Africa. Thirdly, it spread like wildfire. Fourthly, it awakened the Global Church to the very important aspect of her ministry here on Earth: strategic prayer and transformational ministry. Fifthly, it has generated the greatest unity of purpose among God's people over the ages. Sixthly, it has focused attention and prayers on the realities of human society, which constitutes the mission of the church on Earth. Finally, it is preparing the church through its transformational effects for the second advent of the Head of the Church, the Lord Jesus Christ Himself. Brother Graham Power is such a blessing to our generation, the Church in Africa, and the Global Church as a whole.

—REUBEN EZEMADU
CONTINENTAL COORDINATOR
MOVEMENT FOR AFRICAN NATIONAL INITIATIVES (MANI)
INTERNATIONAL DIRECTOR, CMF INC.
MINISTRY CENTER DIRECTOR, DAI
CONTINENTAL COORDINATOR, MANI

If only there were more people with the discipline to seek God's will, the willingness to obey it, and the courage to achieve it with passion! The Global Day of Prayer is a story of God's faithful response to someone who did this very thing. I thank God for Graham Power's obedience to Christ and for the wonderful response that God has brought from it. Today millions of people have been activated for a life of prayer and repentance.

—Mike Bickle
International House of Prayer, Kansas City

The GDOP is an amazing work of grace, birthed in a continent that many would imagine the least likely. This book tells the story of people praying because they refuse to accept the unsatisfactory conditions of the present. Like Abraham of old, "They are looking for a city with foundations, whose Maker and Builder is God." Graham's book is an altar call to prayer. May it inspire you to rebel against the tyranny of things as they are, and to pursue God as you pray for His will to be done on Earth as it is in heaven.

—Moss Ntlha
General Secretary
Evangelical Alliance of South Africa

It is such a joy to serve our Lord in the Global Day of Prayer. Isebel and I praise and thank God for his faithfulness over the years! The story of the Global Day of Prayer is a testimony to the power of God and the dedication and commitment of thousands of volunteers all over the world who do so much to mobilize people for repentance and prayer. May you be blessed and inspired as you read this story!

—Dawie and Isebel Spangenberg
International coordinators for the GDOP

The story of the Global Day of Prayer is one of the most extraordinary parts of God's story in our generation. It is a privilege to be associated with this Holy Spirit-inspired movement, bringing His people together to pray for their nations and our world so that the Earth will be filled with the knowledge of His glory.

—John Robb
Chairman, International Prayer Council

God spoke a word to Graham Power—a word straight from heaven that would cause millions to join together across the nations with one heart, one mind, and in unity of faith in our Lord Jesus Christ in a prayer initiative that was to become the Global Day of Prayer. Because of one man's humility, and one man's obedience to the word of the Lord, the destiny on this present church age has been irrevocably transformed, determining the global harvest for this present and future generations. Graham Power is not only our esteemed ministry colleague, but he is also our very dear friend. He is truly a humble servant of God, our true brother in Christ, and a shining light to this generation. We love him with all our heart.

—RORY AND WENDY ALEC
FOUNDERS OF GOD TV

God is using Graham Power to do something truly remarkable through the Global Day of Prayer. However, it is clear that God wants to do something new—He has said to Graham, "The season for marketplace leaders to impact the world for Christ has begun!"—if only they stay connected to Him in prayer and stay committed to His call! This book tells of the journey to this point, and what God has in store for the next step of the journey.

—REV. CASSIE CARSTENS
AFRICAN LEADERSHIP INSTITUTE FOR COMMUNITY TRANSFORMATION

A few years ago while speaking in Kandy, Sri Lanka, to a group of pastors, they made the comment that they had to be back in their churches in various Sri Lankan cities that weekend because they were all participating in the Global Day of Prayer. I realized afresh that an initiative which started in Africa by a son of Africa had indeed reached the far corners of the Earth. I thank God for Graham's humility and kingdom-mindedness. Let's celebrate the might deeds of the Lord!

—PETER TARANTAL
MANI (MOVEMENT FOR AFRICAN NATIONAL INITIATIVES) SA
COORDINATOR AND WENSA LEADER

Graham is truly an example for all those who call Jesus Lord because of his tireless pursuit of Christ and everything that God is about. We are especially moved by his radically obedient servant's heart, which is a true example of Christ living in and through us. May more in the marketplace answer and obey God's call like Graham has.

—ROY AND YUK LYNN CHEN
MARKETPLACE MINISTERS, HONG KONG

The story of the Global Day of Prayer is a powerful testimony to God's faithfulness and grace in response to a man's courageous obedience! It is God's desire to perform many more miracles of this nature, if only we could find more courageous and obedient Christians. May you be inspired and encouraged as you read this wonderful story!

—REV. DR. DION FORSTER
POWER GROUP/UNASHAMEDLY ETHICAL/GLOBAL DAY OF PRAYER

Acts 19:11 tells us that "God was performing extraordinary miracles by the hands of Paul." Undeniably, God was the source, but Paul was the outlet, for His power to flow and touch not just Paul but everyone in Asia. The Global Day of Prayer is a modern-day extraordinary miracle performed by God, but set in motion by the hands of Graham Power, that has literally touched every nation on Earth. Beginning with one stadium packed with praying people first and unremittingly expanding year after year until the whole world, nation after nation in countless venues, has been united in prayer, the Global Day of Prayer embodies one of the mightiest works of God in our century. But God does not work in a vacuum. He uses people, and this book tells "the story behind the story" that will inspire millions to become God's conduit for extraordinary miracles as Graham Power did. A definite must-read for anyone involved in and thirsting for transformation.

—ED SILVOSO
AUTHOR OF *ANOINTED FOR BUSINESS*
PRESIDENT, INTERNATIONAL TRANSFORMATION NETWORK AND
HARVEST EVANGELISM

When God stirs His people to pray, it is because God is planning to answer! The Global Day of Prayer started by Graham Power is one of God's ways to prepare the church for a *global* awakening. The next great revival will be worldwide. We can only dream about what impact it will have on the nations. Read the story if you want to have faith for the results!

—FLOYD MCCLUNG
ALL NATIONS

It has been such a joy and privilege for our foundation to support the Global Day of Prayer over the last number of years. We thank God for the many miracles and changed lives that have come from this global prayer movement, and we trust the Lord to continue to raise up men and women who will intercede for their families, cities, and nations night and day.

—HANNELI AND HEIN KOEGELENBERG
SOUTH AFRICA

The Global Day of Prayer came like the first Pentecost—as a long expected surprise. For the past two or three decades, the Spirit of God has been stirring His people to pray together and to pray with resolute persistence for Christ's purposes to be fulfilled throughout the Earth. Suddenly, out of Africa came the invitation that had already been resonating in the hearts of millions of believers: to gather as one people before our God in repentance, seeking Him for a great outpouring of His Spirit from heaven so that we will see an even greater ingathering in transformed cities. The story of the Global

Day of Prayer has set our souls on fire with expectancy to see what our God will do to fulfill all that He has promised amidst every people on the face of the Earth.

—STEVE HAWTHORNE
WAYMAKERS

The movement that Graham Power has founded is truly historic. The Global Day of Prayer has helped bring a level of unity in the worldwide church never witnessed before. It is adding to the ocean of prayer building before Christ's return. I don't see GDOP as the end, but just the beginning, of how God is going to use this businessman in the final days.

—MARK ANDERSON
PRESIDENT, GLOBAL PASTORS NETWORK/CALL2ALL

Graham Power is a humble businessman who has been called by God to do a mission that could seem impossible. His mission is to unite Christians worldwide into unified prayer and repentance for the blessing and healing of the nations. This real-life story will unfold how God has used one man to touch the world through the power of the Holy Spirit. After knowing him personally, I have come to find he has been radically obedient when it comes to hearing the voice of God, and because of that obedience this prayer movement amazingly is mission possible!

—CHUCK RIPKA
PRESIDENT, RIPKA ENTERPRISES AND
RIVERCENTER INT'L NETWORK OF CHRISTIANS
AUTHOR, *GOD OUT OF THE BOX*

NOT BY
MIGHT,
NOR BY
POWER

NOT BY
MIGHT,
NOR BY
POWER

GRAHAM POWER
AND DIANE VERMOOTEN

CREATION
HOUSE
A STRANG COMPANY

Not by Might, Nor by Power
by Graham Power and Diane Vermooten
Published by Creation House
A Strang Company
600 Rinehart Road
Lake Mary, Florida 32746
www.creationhouse.com

Unless otherwise noted, all Scripture quotations are from the Holy Bible, New International Version. Copyright © 1973, 1978, 1984, International Bible Society. Used by permission.

Scripture quotations marked AMP are from the Amplified Bible. Old Testament copyright © 1965, 1987 by the Zondervan Corporation. The Amplified New Testament copyright © 1954, 1958, 1987 by the Lockman Foundation. Used by permission.

Scripture quotations marked NKJV are from the New King James Version of the Bible. Copyright © 1979, 1980, 1982 by Thomas Nelson, Inc., publishers. Used by permission.

Design Director: Bill Johnson
Cover design by Amanda Potter

Library of Congress Control Number: 2008912229
International Standard Book Number: 978-1-59979-721-2

First Edition

09 10 11 12 13 — 9 8 7 6 5 4 3 2 1
Printed in the United States of America

Note to the Reader

This is neither the story of a mighty organizational tool nor the abilities of one man, Graham Power. Rather, it is a testimony to the work of the Holy Spirit that began in South Africa and then spread throughout the rest of the world.

ACKNOWLEDGMENTS

I wish to express my sincerest thanks to Graham Power for giving me the opportunity to tell this story on his behalf. Thank you to my husband, Graham, for encouraging me and for always believing in me, and also to my sons, Ryan and Shane, who have always inspired me to tell stories. Finally I wish to thank Anne Warmenhoven who did much of the initial research for this book. I am extremely grateful for her contribution.

—DIANE VERMOOTEN

G OD ALONE KNOWS the internal struggle that I have battled with over the past five years as many people around the globe have encouraged and prompted me to document the Transformation Africa/Global Day of Prayer story, following His clear vision and instructions. In many ways I have felt that as God's vision and plan for GDOP is still very much in the process of "unfolding," it was premature to document it. Moreover, I have been particularly sensitive to the fact that I did not want this blessed miracle of prayer to be seen as "my story." God alone must receive all the glory! This is not man's plan, and no one, least of all I, can claim any credit for what He is unfolding in this delicate process.

When a Coptic Priest in the stillness of the Egyptian desert heard a short description of the vision in 2006, his plea to me was to put this instruction from God into writing so that persons across the world could read and receive the impartation. That was when I knew that the timing and release had come to document the clear instructions from our heavenly Father.

I need to thank so many dedicated intercessors, leaders, patient friends, and family who have coached, mentored, and guided me in the ten years since my "conversion" in 1999. The prayers of Barbara Cilliers, Ayjay Jantjies, and the team of twenty-four dedicated intercessors have been critical in keeping the vision/instruction foremost in my mind. Also, thanks to: the small team of Christian colleagues in the Power Group led by Eleanor Furter and Henrie Jonck who had diligently prayed for my conversion over many years; Mike Winfield, a committed friend in the construction industry; my grandmother and mother who prayed for me throughout my life (my mother is now eighty-four years of age); and the various mentors, especially Adolf Schulz and my pastor Dion Forster, who were key and patient coaches as this wild, young road-building contractor, chasing success in the business world, came to accept Christ.

My love and thanks to Low Bothma, Antinia de Waal, Theo Mayekiso, Dawie and Isebel Spangenberg, Etienne Piek, and all of the dedicated team at the Transformation office who have "offered up their lives" to serve this instruction. To my previous PA, Shelly Kavanagh, and current PA's, Nadene Benvenuti and Melani September, who have never failed to assist me even when the workload is extremely heavy.

I find it difficult to express sufficient thanks to the many intercessors, pastors, and leaders in Cape Town and South Africa who have tirelessly been interceding for our beautiful city and country over the past decades. Their embracing and acceptance of this instruction continues to amaze me. I am convinced that this acceptance can only be as a result of the Holy Spirit's prompting, as you will read in the story that unfolds in the pages of this book.

Many ministries have been significant partners in this move of God. In particular I want to convey immense gratitude to JWIPN (Jericho Walls International Prayer Network), MANI (Movement for African National Initiatives), and the IPC (International Prayer Council).

I thank my amazing, loyal, and dedicated wife, Lauren, who has been a constant source of inspiration and support, even when others doubted the initial instruction. I am truly grateful that God has blessed us with wonderful children: Gary and his wife, Ilene; Nadene and her husband, Stephen; and our youngest daughter, Alaine. They too have been a constant source of strength and encouragement. I regret the years in which I chased after success, and the fact that I wasn't there for them as often as I would have liked to have been. However, I am thankful for their total commitment and love for Christ, and that we as a family have come to jointly accept the calling which God has placed on us.

A special thanks to Anne Warmenhoven who did much of the initial documenting of the facts, and also to Diane Vermooten, a special friend who along with her husband, Graham, and the Media Village team, have been instrumental in producing magnificent video footage as the story of GDOP has unfolded year after year. It was therefore a natural progression to ask Diane to put the story into writing, as she has done so passionately and brilliantly.

May you be encouraged and challenged as you explore this exciting journey with us. God has a special plan for Africa and the world, and I believe we will see much of this unfold in our lifetime. All the glory to Him! May we (and particularly I) remain humble, pray, seek His face, and turn from our wicked ways; and may He forgive our sins and heal our land (2 Chronicles 7:14).

Richest blessings...

—Graham Power
Cape Town, January 2009

CONTENTS

FOREWORD

I FEEL DEEPLY PRIVILEGED to have been asked to write this foreword and commendation of this compelling story of my special friend and partner in the gospel, Graham Power, for this story is a modern–day chapter of the book of Acts. Yes, acts of the Holy Spirit indeed, but also in a sense the acts of a modern-day apostle.

The reality is that Graham Power has manifested the kind of spiritual obedience which one associates with those early apostles and disciples in the first century and has demonstrated the authentic witness and fearless courage which one associates with Christianity's early giants of the faith. Having the humility he does, Graham disclaims anything great or laudatory for himself, and his overriding concern is to give all glory to God, which he does. But the fact remains that the Lord has done something extraordinary through Graham, and as in the first century with Luke the chronicler, it is important that this story also be capably and accurately chronicled. And this Diane Vermooten has most eloquently done. We thank her for this distinguished service.

One of the reasons this chronicling is so very important is not simply to bless many people in the here and now, but that generations to come will know and be inspired and motivated by how the full dedication of one obedient layman was able to touch first his city, then his country, and then the world. In a sense this has been the manifestation of what can happen when a person understands the power, which lies in a deep grasp of instrumentality. Graham has primarily been a class-act example of what being an instrument in the Lord's hands can bring forth. He has kept himself sharp. The Lord has wielded the instrument.

For me, as a friend of Graham's in his journey and as one who has been privileged to encourage him here and there along the way, and for sure been mutually encouraged by him in turn, I feel that the secret in many ways of why the Lord has used him as He has lies in the humble spirit of the man which has produced a passionate eagerness to learn, grow, and deepen in Christ. This has in consequence brought forth in Graham a gentle and compelling openness to his Lord to teach him and guide him both into new truth and into new exploits for the gospel. However, Graham also has a deep openness to his friends as vehicles of mutual encouragement and grace. Graham is therefore not surprisingly always on the growing edge, and this places him constantly on the cutting edge.

I have to say that being invited to be patron of the Transformation Africa Prayer Movement, which has so signally blessed the world, has been for me one of life's most special and humbling privileges. For being identified with the Lord's pressure on His people to pray more resolutely for the advance of His kingdom, the spread of His gospel, and the deepening of His disciples everywhere makes one constantly aware of old shortcomings and new challenges, both in the body of Christ generally and in oneself specifically. And I am sure many readers of this volume will feel similarly challenged, chastened, rebuked, and then inspired to new heights of Christian obedience. So, yes, read and be lifted up to the new place!

The Transformation Africa Prayer Movement, which is extending around the world, also calls each of us to try to grasp what God is saying through all of this. This may not always be easy to discern. However, one cannot but conclude at the very least that our sovereign Lord wants to do something new and fresh among His people and also in the world. First of all, He is calling us to new biblical faithfulness and embracing of the Bible as the fully inspired and authoritative Word of God. Secondly, He is calling us to new unity in His truth, though not at the expense of it. The apostles' doctrine remains vital (Acts 2:42). But we are meant to be "together," as Acts 2:44 reminds us, "All who believed were together" (NKJV). And the Global Days of Prayer have, if nothing else, been extraordinary demonstrations of togetherness. That surely we must seek by all means to perpetuate. Such new unity can also, of course, be the precursor of real revival. And this church desperately needs it if it is to meet the challenges of this troubled world.

Then this movement has produced some wonderful occasions of gospel proclamation. This brings us back in new ways to the great commission as our Lord's major priority, after worship, in His church. Our Lord's last words must surely be our first concern. We are to proclaim the gospel in these very demanding times to the whole world.

Finally, for me at least, the Global Days of Prayer (GDOP) have reminded us that our God wants us to deepen in our discipleship and prayer, individually and corporately. We are not to remain in what Juan Carlos Ortiz once lamented as "the eternal babyhood of the believer."[1] No, we are "to grow up [into]…Christ" (Eph. 4:15, NKJV). Graham and the whole Transformation Africa and GDOP movement have summoned us in new and compelling ways to spiritual adulthood.

So no wonder I praise God for this very special man and his family and colleagues and the movements they have under God spawned for our times. I likewise celebrate Diane's great job and skills, which have produced this volume.

I therefore exhort you to pick up and read and be blessed and challenged into a new day in your own walk with Christ. More than that, this story will put a bomb under your seat, just as watching these events unfold and participating in them in a modest degree over these last years has put one under mine! And for this I thank you, Graham, with all my heart.

Brothers and sisters, our Lord may be coming soon. And some of us may depart this life before then! So let us "work...while it is day; [knowing that] the night is coming when no one can work" (John 9:4, NKJV).

—Dr. Michael Cassidy
December 2008
Pietermaritzburg, Republic of South Africa
Founder, African Enterprise
Patron, the Transformation Africa Prayer Movement

1

THE INSTRUCTION

Write down the revelation and make it plain on
tablets so that a herald may run with it.

—HABAKKUK 2:2

A FAN LAZILY SWUNG back and forth, barely moving the air in the humid room. Sitting upright, Graham blinked rapidly and focused his eyes. Yes, it was the summer of 2000 on the beautiful Spanish island of Mallorca. He slipped his hand under the white sheet, and as he touched Lauren's back he knew that he had to wake her. He had to tell her. His heart was racing. This had not been an ordinary dream, this had been a vision, an instruction, and the clarity with which he recalled every detail created a sense of urgency.

The red light of the digital clock seemed to pierce the darkness. It was 4:00 a.m. Lauren stirred, feeling the intensity of emotion coming from the other side of the bed. What she was about to hear would change the destiny of the Power family and ultimately affect the growth of the Christian prayer movement around the world.

Graham started to recall the details of his dream: "Go back home to the city of Cape Town, South Africa, and hire Newlands Rugby Stadium. Once this venue is secured, invite Christians to gather for a day of repentance and prayer, and then extend an invitation to other cities in South Africa." At first his words were slow and methodical, like one reciting the words of a well-loved poem. But as he recalled the next set of instructions, his voice filled with passion and determination: "Next, the other provinces in the nation are to be challenged, and finally the entire continent of Africa is to be invited to join South Africa in a day of repentance and prayer."

As they sat in the shadowy room discussing the details of these instructions, morning light began to filter through the open windows. A light breeze lowered the temperature. Graham continued to talk of what he had seen and heard in his dream. The words seemed to be tumbling from his lips: stadiums filled to capacity; Christians standing together weeping and praying; people wearing maroon wristbands; small "goodie" bags filled with a drink and a snack. The purpose for the meeting was clear—this was to be a time for repentance and prayer.

Lauren was not used to hearing Graham talk of "stadiums filled with praying Christians." In 1983, they had started Power Construction, which had since grown into one of the largest privately owned civil construction companies in southern Africa. She had often heard her husband discuss plans to build national roads, shopping centers, golf estates, and housing complexes, but this was different. Silently she listened, and she hid these things in her heart because it all seemed so unusual. And if any of these things were to actually happen, then surely it would be God. Leaning back against the headboard, she closed her eyes and smiled, thinking how unusual it was for Graham to remember so many details. Yes, there was something very different about this dream.

2

THE VISION

See, the former things have taken place, and new things I declare;
before they spring into being I announce them to you.

—ISAIAH 42:9

T HE WEATHER HAD been windy and misty for more than a week, so
typical of the Cape in winter. Weather reports were not encouraging,
and there was little hope that the cold front would move away from
Cape Aghulhas for several days. Aghulhas is the southernmost tip of
Africa and, unlike the majestic Cape Point, has no peaks or ragged cliffs
to entice tourists to photograph the beauty and splendor. Rather in an
undramatic manner, Africa just seems to slip into the ocean, marked by
nothing more than a solitary lighthouse.

This was the final destination for a group of approximately fifty Youth
With A Mission staff and students. They were part of a prayer move that
would pray from the cardinal points of every continent. In Africa, teams
had gone to Senegal in the west, Tunisia in the north, and Ethiopia in the
east. The main focus of their prayers was the spiritual and physical needs
of Africa. Small groups huddled together on the pebbled beaches. Occa-
sionally a gust of wind would carry the words of the young intercessors
out to sea, and even those standing closest could not hear what was being
prayed. Despite the difficult situation, these prayers were being heard and
recorded in the heavenlies.

The hours moved on, and as the clouds began to threaten rain, the
leader of the group grabbed a twisted piece of driftwood and started
drawing the shape of Africa on the pebbled beach. Others soon joined the
action and covered the outline with pieces of seaweed. The long tentacles
quickly resembled Africa, and the young men and women moved along
the borders praying for this continent. Then as quickly as the storm clouds
had gathered, they moved away. Under the expanse of a gray, African sky,
a voice called out from the crowd, "If my people, who are called by my
name, will humble themselves and pray and seek my face and turn from
their wicked ways, then will I hear from heaven and will forgive their sin
and will heal their land" (2 Chron. 7:14).

No sooner had these words been prayed than an elderly lady moved to the bottom of the map and stood on the place that denoted Cape Town. She was wearing a red scarf, and taking the scarf off her neck, she began to move across the continent. Wildly waving her hands in the air, the red material moved in the wind like a flame. She was enacting the vision that God had burned into her mind that a spark would begin to burn in the city of Cape Town and very quickly would become a holy fire across Africa.

This vision was not a new vision, because for nearly one hundred years God had been giving this picture to believers all around the world. The details may have differed slightly, but the core truth was always the same. The message was clear—Africa would become a light to the world, and a new revival would start at the tip of Africa and move across the continent.

Some of the first recordings of these prophetic messages can be traced back to 1910. Stories are told of a young man in Sweden disrupting a traditional morning service when he stood and described to the people a vision he was receiving from God. He had seen a revival starting at the tip of Africa and spreading over the entire continent.

Some decades later the founder of All Nations Gospel Publishers woke in the early hours of the morning. He could clearly see a map of the world on his bedroom wall. Gazing at the map he was surprised when suddenly the southern tip of Africa burst into flames. It only took a few minutes and the entire continent was ablaze.

While these visions had all been pointers toward a move of God that would start at the tip of Africa, there is little doubt that men such as Andrew Murray (1828–1917) and William Duma (1907–1977) played a foundational role in chartering the history of South Africa's prayer movement.

As a minister of the Dutch Reformed Church of Wellington (South Africa), Andrew Murray had a vision of winning Africa for Christ. This vision motivated his desire to pray and live a life that was totally surrendered to God. In his book *With Christ in the School of Prayer*, Murray presents New Testament teaching on prayer and encourages the reader to move past simplistic prayers that are ineffectual. He longed that the church would know that "God rules the world by the prayers of His saints, that prayer is the power by which Satan is conquered, and that by prayer the church on earth has disposal of the powers of the heavenly world."[1] Firmly living out this belief, Murray inspired the church to access the powers of heaven through prayer and to bring the gospel to the world through the power of the Holy Spirit.

Murray's words were great seeds planted in the history of the prayer movement. Much fruit would be seen in following generations. His personal vision of "Africa for Christ" would eventually become the mission statement for the Transformation Africa prayer movement.

As a young boy living on the beautiful green rolling hills of Natal (KwaZulu-Natal, South Africa), the young William Duma was fascinated with God's Creation. He would sit on the red ground outside his family kraal, which was made from sticks woven together and plastered with mud and earth. Looking up at the great African sky, which seemed to have no end, he acknowledged the "Great One."[2]

His hunger for intimacy with God led to his conversion as a teenager. After God miraculously healed Duma, he dedicated his life to a ministry of prayer, intercession, and healing. God began to use this man at the time in South Africa's history when apartheid was not just lived in the political and social domains of society, but sadly also in the church.

Despite social norms and laws, Duma carried the presence of God into the heart of the church. As the power of his ministry and the obvious impact of a life lived in prayer became evident, Duma's ministry grew until thousands of lives were changed and people began to follow his lead of "praying without ceasing." (See 1 Thessalonians 5:17.) Duma's prayer life would often include days of 24/7 prayer. His followers wondered when he ever slept. The name *Duma* means "thunder," and the echo of those thunderous prayers for the salvation of souls and for the people of Africa still can be heard today.[3]

These men are just two of many whom God used to paint the backdrop for the spiritual revivals of 1860 and 1905. Prevailing prayer was integral to both of these revivals. Despite these times of great spiritual sensitivity in a nation where leaders were willing to acknowledge the presence of God, South Africa then created a legal system that devalued the God-derived dignity of people, classing them according to the color of their skin. It was called apartheid and it would last for more than forty years.

> Some people pray just to pray and some people pray to know God.[4]
> —Andrew Murray

Apartheid is an Afrikaans word meaning "separate,"[5] and so successful was this form of governance that people lived separate lives, with no reason to cross the great color divide. Formulated in 1948, apartheid was the legal government of the nation until 1994. Those forty-plus years were turbulent ones in the history of South Africa. Many inhumane deeds were done, some even in the name of God and the church. For fear of being labeled as "political," the church for the most part was silent. Looking back, it could be said that the silence was in fact deafening. But God had not forgotten the prayers of His people as they cried to Him for mercy and deliverance.

Confidence in South Africa's ability to lift herself from the constraints of apartheid were low, the economy was sliding, and fear was a constant companion to people from every racial group. It was in this time of despair that the body of Christ began standing in the gap for the nation. In May 1990, a Xhosa pastor from the Transkei called the first national forty-day fast. It was here, as people waited on God, knowing that the situation was hopeless, that God clearly spoke from the book of Isaiah, "Can a country be born in a day or a nation be brought forth in a moment?" (Isa. 66:8).

This was the word that spurred the church onward to believe that a new South Africa, a new nation, could be birthed and that God wanted His church to pray and believe in Him for the *kairos* moment in the land. South Africa, a country of promise, of rich inheritance, was a nation ready to be brought forth. As prayer initiatives sprang up around the country, Christians started to believe that with God the impossible could become the possible.

By the end of 1993, South Africa stood on the verge of her first democratic elections. But despite the political significance of this watershed moment, frustration was high in the black communities and morale low in white communities. The future was unclear. Questions and doubts plagued the business community: Would the economy withstand a new government? Would a black government simply turn the tables on the white community? Would violence escalate and security deteriorate?

Many professionals had already left the country in an exodus that became known as the brain drain. In the midst of this time of uncertainty, it was the body of Christ that played an instrumental role in the peaceful transition to democracy in the 1994 elections.

It was under the spiritual leadership of Dr. Michael Cassidy, founder of African Enterprise, that thousands gathered in a stadium in Natal to pray for peace. It was with godly wisdom and insight that Dr. Cassidy and other Christian leaders negotiated for peaceful elections and community support from all peoples. The world expected a bloodbath, but the church became galvanized to pray. Media teams from every major network around the world descended on the country, but as millions of people stood in long lines waiting to cast the first vote of their lives, it soon became evident that a miracle was happening. Within twenty-four hours, media teams were called home because there was no story.

How wrong they were, because this was in fact the greatest story of all. This was God answering the cries of His children; this was the church assuming its rightful position as intercessor and gatekeeper for the nation. This was a miracle in our time.

3
AFRICA'S PAIN

You who call on the LORD, *give yourselves no rest, and give him no rest till he establishes Jerusalem and makes her the praise of the earth.*
—ISAIAH 62:6–7

FOR CENTURIES AFRICA has carried the disparaging title of "The Dark Continent." This title denoted not only the skin color of most of the African people, but also the fear and the mystery of unexplored and undiscovered Africa. While European explorers were colonizing the world, much of Africa was still unknown until the final decades of the nineteenth century. The African landscape had kept the adventuresome explorers at bay for hundreds of years. Africa has some of the harshest deserts on earth: the Sahara in the north, and the Namib and Kalahari in the south. The eastern regions of the continent feature the Great African Rift Valley, making the area difficult to reach. Not only was Africa breathtakingly beautiful, but also in many cases it was impenetrable.

Any reading of the history of this continent and its people includes bloodstained punctuation marks, years of colonization, millions of lives sold as slaves, genocide, war, and famine. The African story has been told in pain, but through the misery there has always been a song of hope; a deep, burning desire that Africa's time would finally come and that there would be an opportunity to break the chains of bondage; a time when Africa would become the bearer of light and no longer carry the burden of darkness. In Celtic, *Africa* means "pleasant," and in Irish, "agreeable," but all too often Africa has not lived the blessing of her name.

The 1994 elections had come and gone without much incident; a new government was in place, and many of the fears imagined never became a reality. Yet despite the euphoria of the fledging democracy, South Africa was neither pleasant nor agreeable by the late 1990s. Democracy had given the majority of South Africans the right to vote but had not put an end to the corruption, violence, and rape that threatened the nation's survival. Once again morale plummeted, and hopelessness became the pervading tone of most conversation.

It was during this time of fear that all around the nation, local and national prayer initiatives began to remind themselves of God's promise from Isaiah, "Can a country be born in a day or a nation be brought forth in a moment?" (Isa. 66:8). Believers started to pray with a new fervor and determination, intentionally turning to God in prayer, wanting to access the powers of heaven for the transformation of South Africa and all of Africa.

In the Western Cape where most commuters travel by taxi, the taxi wars were escalating. These wars were the fights between taxi associations and individual minibus taxi drivers.

At the same time an organization called PAGAD (People Against Gangs and Drugs) began to fight against the high incidence of drugs and gangsterism among the young people of Cape Town. Originally started as an interfaith civic group, their ranks soon became infiltrated by fundamentals and radicals. As the group began to move toward militancy, Christians and moderate peace-loving members began to distance themselves from the organization. The first series of bombs were intended to warn and frighten drug dealers. Later the bombs were laced with nails and sharp objects that killed and maimed innocent people.

Through the late 1990s, twenty-two bombs exploded, killing and maiming hundreds of men, women, and children who happened to be in the path of this nameless cruelty. Ordinary citizens became fearful, numerous lives were lost, and as chaos ruled the streets the church continued to pray.

Eddie Edison, a pastor from a poor community on the Cape Flats, had firsthand experience of this tragedy, as he lived in the heart of the troubled areas. But Eddie also had knowledge of a God who promised that if His people humbled themselves and prayed, He would hear from heaven and heal their land. (See 2 Chronicles 7:14.) With this verse motivating his actions, Pastor Edison invited a small group of Christians to join him in prayer.

Sitting on the hard benches of a church hall, these men and women prayed for hours, begging God to intervene and to start fulfilling all the prophetic words that had been given to the nation. Rev. Trevor Pearce, an Anglican minister who had also grown up during the apartheid years, started joining these prayer meetings. Trevor was often instrumental in pushing the boundaries of preconceived ideas and challenging Christians to defy the status quo and walk in dignity. He was no stranger to the pain and hardship of discrimination and violence, yet his gentle disposition was often used by God to fulfill the role of peacemaker. To many, Trevor became known as the "man of peace."

By 1998, stories of violence and interest rates of 25 percent were regular headlines on the front pages of South African newspapers. This was also the year that Trevor Pearce accepted an invitation to be a delegate at a Sharing of Ministries Abroad (SOMA) retreat in Richmond, Virginia.

It was at this conference that he heard a new story that gripped his heart and mind. Retreat director John Guernsey told the miraculous story of God at work in the city of Cali, Columbia. Reports of saved lives, community transformation, and national influence seemed to resound so deeply in Trevor's heart that he felt broken, thinking of his own homeland. Was it possible that South Africa could ever experience this kind of transformation?

He sat and listened to every word, not missing a detail of the incredible story. It felt as though the words were exploding into his soul, and in an instant he knew that God was birthing something of such importance and significance that he could not wait to return home. He was burning with a desire to ignite the flame, inspire his people, and believe that the Cali, Columbia, miracle could become a South African miracle as well.

Flying home to South Africa, Pearce fiercely guarded his most prized treasures—an audio copy of the retreat and a bound copy of the soon-to-be-published book *Informed Intercessions* by George Otis, Jr. This documented account of the Cali, Columbia, story also included principles for successful community transformation.

Trevor wasted absolutely no time in meeting with Eddie Edison, who was already praying with a group of seventy pastors for the city and the nation. As the group listened to the recorded voice of George Otis and watched the stories of transformation and redemption, they too felt that deep stirring deep within their hearts. There seemed to be so many similarities between the two countries. Drugs, death, and despair had all been part of daily life for the residents of Cali, Columbia, until the Holy Spirit brought transformation through the praying church. What Satan had intended for evil, God was using for good.

There was a growing air of expectation as churches, home cells, prisons, and leaders began to watch and listen to the Cali, Columbia, story. The numerous intercessory groups who had already been praying for transformation in South Africa felt energized, and they increased their time spent in prayer. They asked God to raise up the church to be an instrument of change. They begged for God to lead the way and to put the right people in place—men and women who were willing to lead. They asked and trusted God for a miracle.

Over the next two years it seemed as though there was a rumbling of intercessory prayer at a grassroots level, and at this time the CTCT (Cape Town Community Transformation) was formed. Every time these Christians gathered to pray, their numbers grew—firstly from the 1,200 intercessors who gathered in the Lighthouse to the 5,000 who stood on the cobbled streets of the Grand Parade in Cape Town.

These meetings galvanized a critical mass in the city, and the stage was set for the transformation movement that would soon explode from the tip of Africa.

4

A SEED IS SOWN

"Come, follow me," Jesus said, "and I will make you fishers of men."
—MATTHEW 4:19

OXFORD STREET IS a long road in an ordinary middle-class suburb of Cape Town. It is lined with tall trees that cast dappled shadows on the black tar surface every afternoon just before the sun sets. This shadowy road was the playground for the young Graham Power and his siblings.

Never could one have imagined that the toy trucks they played with on this road would one day become the powerful Caterpillar construction trucks of the Power Group of Companies. Graham was one of five children. His family home was a modest house in a small community on the outskirts of Cape Town. Finding a place of solitude in the house was difficult as every room was a perpetual hive of activity. Laughter and noise were the glue that kept the family together. Mr. Alan Power was a gifted musician who worked as a motor mechanic. His limited income did not allow for all the children to complete secondary schooling. As the older children finished grade ten at the young age of only fifteen, they were forced to leave school so that the younger ones could continue their schooling and complete grade twelve.

Church attendance was the Sunday morning activity for most South African families, and once the perfunctory duty was over, the reality of Christ made little or no impact on life for the rest of the week. The Power family regularly attended church. Alan Power, who was a second-generation South African of Irish descent, attended the local Catholic Church, and Ernesta Power would faithfully worship at the Dutch Reformed Church. Choosing which church to attend was not a difficult decision for Graham, then a teenager. It was easily determined by the youth group or church attended by the prettiest girls.

It was at this time that Cape Town churches were all working together to fill a local sports stadium for a citywide rally with Nicky Cruz. Billboards invited young people to come and hear the story of the man featured in the popular movie *The Cross and the Switchblade*.

It was not the advertising that enticed Graham to attend this rally, but the invitation of a young girlfriend's family. As the streams of young people walked into the stadium, the young Graham walked beside his girlfriend and was impressed with the number of people attending this Christian rally.

Nicky Cruz took the microphone, and with a confidence birthed out of his personal faith in Jesus Christ, told a crowd of about four thousand people the story of his conversion. Stories of an abusive family, brutal activities within the Mau Mau gang, one of the most vicious Puerto Rican gangs in New York City during the 1950s and 60s, and then his meeting with David Wilkerson, the evangelist, filled the stadium. As the crowd sat in silence, enthralled with his honesty and the faithfulness of God toward this violent gang member, Graham listened to every word and felt his heart stir.

As the rally came to an end, Nicky Cruz moved to the edge of a trailer that was the improvised stage, and as the bright lights of the stadium pierced the warm balmy darkness, he extended an invitation for people to give their lives to Jesus. Graham felt the prompting of the Holy Spirit. Cautiously looking around, he became filled with fear, fear of what others would think. Desperately wanting to stand, he watched hundreds of young people go to the front for salvation and prayer, but still he sat. He was feeling the call of obedience, and his heart was with the young men and women who were receiving counseling and prayer, but he never moved.

As the crowd began to leave Green Point stadium, Graham sensed a heaviness in his heart. This was the first time he had been to a crusade or heard such a clear presentation of the message of salvation, but on this occasion he did not respond. While the words of the message had been sealed in his heart, the desire to respond soon passed, and Graham set out on a path in the pursuit of personal wealth, happiness, and fulfillment.

This journey of finding meaning and worth was fueled by this young man's passion for success and recognition. After completing one year of military service for a nation that used conscription to build the national army, he joined a civil engineering company working as a learner construction surveyor and set himself stringent achievement goals.

Determined to achieve these goals by sheer hard work, Graham worked long hours; he studied harder than his colleagues, continually checked his projections, and quickly found favor with his superiors. He caught the attention of his supervisors, and by the age of twenty-one became the youngest site agent in the company. It seemed as though he had discovered the formula for success and fulfillment.

Despite the long work hours, Graham still found time to go to the parties where his friends would meet and socialize. Then one night at his younger brother's fourteenth birthday party, he looked across the room and saw a young woman a few years his junior. He immediately was attracted to this fifteen-year-old girl with a shy smile and gentle spirit.

Asking a few questions, he soon discovered that this was Lauren Baumker. Her parents were in the hotel industry. Her mother was of British descent, but her father was a man of German heritage who would accept nothing but the best for his daughter. The determined Graham knew that he would meet those expectations and be the best for Lauren.

Their friendship soon developed into a romantic relationship, and as Graham began to get more responsibility within the company, he was required to work on projects several hours from Lauren who was at a finishing school in Port Elizabeth nearly eight hundred kilometers away. The commute finally just got to be too much, and Graham decided that after three years of dating he was ready to marry Lauren.

Once married, the young couple established their first home on the west coast of South Africa in the small community town of Vredenburg. The internal drive that motivated Graham to succeed at a young age kept growing, and having tasted the pleasure of success, he was determined to get more.

He recognized the opportunity for young entrepreneurs who were determined and focused on success. This determination saw Graham moving from surveyor to contracts manager with six to eight projects under his leadership. Each promotion brought more responsibility and financial reward. In only nine-and-a-half years he had climbed the corporate ladder and was ready for an even bigger challenge.

Graham and Lauren started discussing the possibility of starting their own company. At first the idea seemed impossible; they had a young family and very little finances, but Lauren kept encouraging Graham to open his own company. He was working such long hours, and she felt that their family could directly benefit from his hard work and determination. Lauren kept prompting her husband to take the risk, and his father-in-law began to give him advice on business management and even made a capital investment into the young startup company. Together they finally made the decision to start out on their own business. And, so, the Power Construction Company was born.

The young family moved onto the foothills of the beautiful Sir Lowry's pass, on a farm called Elandskloof. The white house was designed in the traditional Cape Dutch style, with the high gables over the main entrance, and a row of horse stables along the back of the house.

A few easy alterations converted those stables into the Power Company offices. Both Graham and Lauren worked passionately in the company, which at this stage had only one vehicle, a small orange pick-up truck and one staff member. Years later, as the company grew, their logo would include a bright orange square as a reminder of their small beginnings. Civil construction engineering was not an easy area to break into as the contracts are usually extremely large and the amount of capital needed to finance the building of roads, townships, and shopping centers is vast. Despite this handicap, Graham's reputation for hard work, excellence, and good decision-making preceded him, and one project at a time the company began to grow.

The more success the business had, the more the Power family was able to change their lifestyle. Success bred more success. Before long Graham was well on his way to wealth and public recognition. In 1989, only six years after starting his own business, Graham was awarded the South African Junior (under forty years of age) Businessman of the Year Award from the Johannesburg Chamber of Business. Not long after that he was presented with the prestigious President's Award from the SA Institute for Civil Engineers, for Meritorious Service for his work in Labor Intensive Construction. Considering the fact that Graham had neither an engineering nor a business degree made this achievement even more notable. The cycle of instant fulfillment, bigger cars, more game farms, another boat, another house, bigger and better, soon began to spiral around the family.

Graham was getting what he thought he wanted. Now he had all the things he had dreamed of as he grew up, but as soon as he managed to acquire the new possessions, they lost their luster and allure. There was an emptiness that could not be filled, and every now and then the echo of childhood laughter filled his mind. He remembered the time when his family barely had money for clothing and school fees, but a time when they had each other and they had happiness; now he could afford to buy most of the things his heart desired, but slowly he began to lose his family.

The more success he attained, the more Lauren watched her husband disappear into a fog of meetings, business lunches, and work. And as he climbed the ladder, Lauren was left alone at home with their three young children. Work consumed his time. He became an absent father, and yet still he searched for that illusive something that he hoped and believed would ultimately bring satisfaction.

Unbeknown to Graham, there had been a group of Christians in his company who had closely watched his lifestyle and his determination to succeed. "Surely," they thought, "if God would intervene in Mr. Power's life, and if all the energy he used to pursue success could be put into kingdom activities, the impact would be great." This small group of believers led by Graham's secretary, Eleanor Furter, and a young engineer within the company, Henri Jonck, started meeting early in the morning to pray for the Power Company, and particularly for Graham Power.

One evening after everyone had left the offices, Henri walked quietly down the corridor toward Graham's office. His heart had become burdened for the owner of the company. Standing in the empty and silent office he took a small bottle of oil from his pocket and anointed the doorframe, begging God to save Graham Power and to redirect his life toward Himself.

Things seemed to improve in the company when a few months later, Henri was given permission to hold lunchtime meetings for anyone interested in hearing a gospel message.

Graham was certainly not opposed to these meetings, because he thought it always helped to have a little religion in the hearts of your workers. In his experience religion made workers more faithful and hardworking. The only condition to the meetings was that these prayer times could not detract from work time, and if anyone returned to work late as a result of these meetings they would have to work the time back in. Results were important and time was money.

As the number of people attending these meetings began to grow, so did the intensity of the prayer for the salvation of everyone in the company.

Graham would sometimes slip into the back of the meeting to hear what was being said. Sitting in the last row he would listen to the speakers bringing their message of hope, and then just before the meeting ended he would slip out of the hall and return to his desk. It pleased him to see so many people wanting to "get some God." But nothing he heard at those meetings turned his heart or made him feel that same intensity of emotion he felt years earlier on the night he heard Nicky Cruz ask people to give their lives to Christ. Suddenly those days seemed a long way away; in fact, it could have been in a different lifetime.

5

THE INVITATION

Listen, O heavens, and I will speak; hear, O earth, the words of my
mouth. Let my teaching fall like rain and my words descend like dew,
like showers on new grass, like abundant rain on tender plants.
—DEUTERONOMY 32:1–2

B
Y 1998 THE political and economic climate of the nation seemed to have dropped to an all-time low, and morale was declining. Still the Christians kept praying, believing that God had brought the country far, so surely He would not abandon it now.

As despair increased, a handful of city businessmen started holding seminars and meetings, inviting their colleagues to meet in small cell groups for prayer and intercession. They encouraged their colleagues to be bold in their faith and to trust God for miraculous answers to prayers. Options for a brighter tomorrow were rapidly declining, and the prophetic words about the nation still remained unfilled.

For several years Graham kept receiving invitations to attend Christian businessmen's breakfasts. Repeatedly he declined the invitation but finally relented when Mike Winfield, a competing contractor, personally invited him to attend yet another breakfast. Graham agreed to make a concerted effort to attend. The motivation for attending was not necessarily to hear a God message, but to network with other businessmen and to see if there were any more opportunities for good contacts or possibilities for new business deals.

On the day that Mike called, Graham realized that the venue for the breakfast was close to his home, so he decided to accept the invitation. Checking his diary, he confirmed that both dates were available. He penciled in the breakfast appointments and made a mental note of the guest speakers' names.

One name was quite familiar to him, but the other was a name he had not heard before. The first breakfast meeting was to be addressed by Michael Cassidy of African Enterprise. Michael Cassidy was well known in both the political and religious circles of South Africa. It was Michael who, on the invitation of Nelson Mandela, helped to broker peace in

South Africa's transition into democracy. He had already addressed parliamentarians from New Zealand to England and Ireland, Zimbabwe, and Uganda. Around the world, God had already used this man as a peacemaker and messenger for God's heart for peace, justice, and reconciliation. Now it was South Africa's time.

Graham attended the first breakfast at the Lord Charles Hotel in Somerset West. As he sat in the beautifully decorated room, he looked around, noticing how Michael Cassidy's message held the attention of every businessman and woman. As he listened, Graham was challenged by the clear message of the gospel and the story of a God who loved him, died on the cross for him, and had a purpose and plan for his life.

About four months later, Peter Pollock was the speaker at the second breakfast. Peter Pollock was an icon in the cricket world. As one of the nation's best fast bowlers, Peter Pollock was a household name for most South African families. Peter Pollock, much like Graham Power, had been seeking for fulfillment in the acclamations of the sporting world, and despite being hailed as the country's best, he was still on a personal pilgrimage looking for meaning, worth, and fulfillment. Peter's wife had closely followed Christ for a long time, and her life was an example of what it meant to live a life totally surrendered to God. Late one Sunday night in an undramatic way, Peter Pollock, sitting at home mindlessly watching television, heard a salvation message, and in an instant he discovered Truth.

A few years later when his professional cricket career came to an end, Peter dedicated his life to telling others of his miraculous conversion and of the secret of being successful on and off the cricket field.

Being a man of his word, Graham kept his commitment and attended the second breakfast. As he parked his car and walked into the crowded room, he remembered the words he had heard at the previous breakfast when Michael Cassidy had so clearly presented a message of salvation and hope.

The breakfast plates were still been cleared away when Peter Pollock took to the podium and started telling his life's story. His words were honest and sincere. He shared about an external life that was captured in international newspapers and sporting broadcasts, but about an internal life that was empty and void. He had worldly recognition but no security. Graham leaned forward and listened closely to every word. It seemed to him as though Peter was telling his own story. Suddenly he felt as though he understood the dilemma raging in his own heart and mind.

When the message came to an end, Peter Pollock asked the room full of businessmen to consider his message and to accept Christ. Graham very tentatively prayed the Sinner's Prayer and asked God to forgive his sins and to change his life. As he silently prayed, he realized that he was responding to the same invitation he had heard Nicky Cruz present all those years ago, the one that he declined in Green Point Stadium at the age of seventeen.

It was only later that Graham realized that there were people watching closely to see who raised their hand, so that they could contact the men and do follow-up calls.

The word was quick to circulate in the Christian community. Graham Power had prayed the Sinner's Prayer. Immediately realizing that their prayers had been answered, the men and women of Power Construction who had been praying for Graham's salvation at office headquarters began to pray for true discipleship to happen. Graham never mentioned this decision to Lauren and his family because he still needed to be sure about what he had done.

It was several weeks later when Graham returned to the office after the Christmas break that he received an unusual phone call. The caller identified himself as Adolf Schultz. He said that he had seen Graham at the businessmen's breakfast and wanted to invite Graham to be the guest speaker at another businessmen breakfast. Glancing down at his diary, Graham saw the date in question was open, so he accepted the appointment.

It was only after he agreed to talk that he inquired about the topic. To his surprise the topic for the morning was "Christianity in the Workplace." Taking a pen, Graham jotted down the date, time, and venue. As he wrote he wondered what on earth he was doing. He certainly was not in a position to discuss Christianity in the workplace. He hardly knew how to live as a Christian, and how this faith was to be lived out in the workplace was something he had never even thought about. He felt uneasy as he contemplated the subject for the morning. Suddenly he needed an out, a reason to decline the invitation and still save face.

Hope came when he realized that the twenty-fourth of February was the most likely date for the next monthly meeting of the South African Federation for Civil Engineering Contractors (SAFCEC). As president of the federation, Graham knew that he would have no option but to attend. He greeted Adolf, put down the phone, and thought that as soon as the committee date was confirmed he would call and cancel this breakfast. He let out a soft sigh of relief; at least this was the escape that he silently prayed for.

The days passed and for some unknown reason the SAFCEC date was never confirmed. With the breakfast drawing nearer and no reason not to go, Graham began to panic.

His driven sense of excellence knew he had to speak with conviction and passion, but his heart knew that the words he would speak would surely sound empty and lack authenticity. He did not know how to be a Christian in the workplace. In fact he was not even sure if it were possible to be a true Christian, to follow biblical guidelines, and still be successful in business.

The following Sunday, Graham attended church, and as soon as the service was over he stopped and had a word with his pastor, Dion Forster. He needed help. Dion, like many others, had heard of Graham's prayer at the Pollock breakfast. When Graham turned to him for advice on what books to read in preparation for his message, Dion knew this was the time to make a decision. Right there and then he determined in his heart that he would not only be a pastor to Graham Power but that he would also be a friend and a guide for Graham on his journey of discovery with God.

Dion gave Graham two books and told him he would be willing to discuss the contents of the books at any time. For the next two weeks Graham found himself compelled to read every word on the pages of the books he had been given. He read the Bible with new understanding and became frantic in his attempt to gain insight. Hour after hour he would read and study. And as he read, the Holy Spirit worked in his life and began renewing this self-made man.

Suddenly the reality of what a life surrendered to God meant became crystal clear. He knew he had no option; this was his moment of accountability before the living God. At just before 11:00 p.m. on February 20, 1999, Graham Power knelt down on the floor of his study and totally committed his life to Christ.

In that quiet moment the truth was revealed. All the worldly success would amount to nothing; the highest acclaim of business had left him at the lowest place before the cross. As he knelt on the tile floor, he experienced a deep and satisfying sense of peace as never before. In an instant it felt as though the chasing had ended, and the race was over. The puzzle pieces had fallen into place.

Graham stayed on the floor for a long time and settled his account with God. From that moment forward he would live his life totally dedicated to God and his beloved family, and he would reposition his company in accordance with godly principles. Never again would his faith be a worship of convenience but rather a 24/7 dedication to God. This meant that he would live a life governed by God's principles twenty-four hours a day, seven days a week. This was the moment of total dedication and commitment.

Four days later he would not only present a talk on Christianity in the workplace, but he would also have to begun to experience the reality of Christ in his life.

Getting up from the floor, Graham knew with assurance that this time there was no going back, no more reluctant or silent prayers; this was a faith step that would have to be lived out from this moment forward. He knew that Lauren would have to be the first

> But those who wait for the Lord [who expect, look for, and hope in Him] shall change and renew their strength and power; they shall lift their wings and mount up [close to God] as eagles [mount up to the sun]; they shall run and not be weary, they shall walk and not faint or become tired.
> —Isaiah 40:31, AMP

person to know about this important decision. Closing his books, turning off the lights, and quietly shutting the study door, Graham Power left his old life behind and walked toward his bedroom a new man.

It was nearly midnight by the time he entered his room. He could see Lauren sound asleep and decided not to wake her, as he was not exactly sure of what to say. He needed time to internalize this new decision. He waited almost ten days to tell Lauren about the most important decision of his life.

This was the night—with his children's earthly inheritance secured— that the incredible legacy of his life finally began.

Graham knew that he would need to be guided along this new road. He needed someone to direct his course in the early days of personally knowing God. His pastor and friend, Dion Forster, was true to his commitment to serve the Power family and soon started meeting with Graham and Lauren every week. In the privacy of their own home for nearly six months they were able to study together and search for God's answers to the questions that had so radically changed the direction of their lives.

6
HOPE IS BORN

1 knew that this was the word of the LORD.
—JEREMIAH 32:8

THE CONSEQUENCES OF Graham's decision to dedicate his business to the Lord were immediately felt by the Power Company. Within weeks many discussions were held at various levels of leadership about previously held business principles and practices and how they would be changed so that Power Construction could be run on biblical principles.

An ethics committee was formed, and this small team put every aspect of the company's policies and procedures under the biblical microscope. It was not plain sailing as Graham was still responsible to his directors and had to move forward with the support of the team.

At one meeting the atmosphere was fairly tense, and directors and shareholders challenged Graham, saying that his ideas of ethical business were tantamount to suicide for the company. It was at this meeting that Graham made the final decision regarding his company and his faith. If the directors could not accept his leadership toward a biblical company, he would exit the business, even though he was the majority shareholder with 80 percent of the company's outstanding stock. This was not an ultimatum; this was Graham cementing the primacy of God in his personal life and that of the Power Group of Companies.

Graham was no longer afraid of what others would think; he was determined to lead his company on a new path. He devoured any literature or guidance that he could get on the repositioning of his company. The books *Half Time* by Bob Buford and *Jesus CEO* by Laurie Beth Jones seemed to speak directly to this need.

As he read *Anointed for Business* by Ed Silvoso, he began to fully understand his role as a marketplace minister. Graham realized that he now had a responsibility toward the men and women who worked at Power Construction, and the truth of the fact grew on him. Graham knew that he was a marketplace minister, he was anointed for business, and that he would use his company for the extension of the kingdom of God.

Concepts such as firstfruits, tithing, and prayer evangelism were all new ideas to this man who at a moment in time had turned all the energy he had used to become successful into becoming significant.

With so much to learn, Graham would drive to the office early in the morning and wait on God for guidance in regards to company decisions, contracts, and even staff needs.

Adolf Schultz, the man who had extended the original invitation to speak at the breakfast, approached Graham and made a commitment to disciple him. For nearly two years, Adolf and Graham met from six to seven every Monday morning and together studied the Word of God.

These early morning hours of prayer became the firstfruits of Graham's time. He wanted to know the mind of Christ, and the only way he could discover biblical truths was to spend time in the Word.

In the months that followed, Graham realized that prayer was only part of his responsibility, and that as a Christian in a nation where vast majorities of the people live in abject poverty, he needed to play an important role in the uplifting of underprivileged people.

Reading Proverbs 3:9–10, "Honor the LORD with your wealth, with the firstfruits of all your crops; then your barns will be filled to overflowing, and your vats will brim over with new wine," Graham felt his heart stir. God was giving him understanding and strategies. He determined then and there to establish a trust fund where 10 percent of the profits made from each of the twelve companies in the Power Group were accumulated. This fund is used to support the work of social programs around the country. The critical issues of HIV/AIDS, education, and feeding programs receive special attention.

It was in one of those early mornings alone with the Lord, before the start of another hectic day, that Graham read Deuteronomy 8:17–18: "You may say to yourself, 'My power and the strength of my hands have produced this wealth for me.' But remember the LORD your God, for it is he who gives you the ability to produce wealth, and so confirms his covenant."

These words cut deep into his heart and soul. For over twenty years he had taken the full credit for his success and the vast accumulation of his wealth; now he began to realize that it was God who had given him his health and the talents and ability to produce his wealth. The full realization of the fact also dawned on him that the Power Group of Companies was not just a means to get rich but was a company that had a crucial role to play in changing the spiritual climate of not just South Africa but also Africa.

The needs of the nation were great, and combating crime, violence, and poverty seemed like a daunting challenge, but Graham intentionally determined that his company was going to be part of the solution and that he would follow God's blueprint for transformation. Graham, in conjunction with directors, set a vision statement for the company that stated their calling was "to improve the lives of the people in Africa, through infrastructure development."

As a young believer Graham had no idea on how to bring about transformation, but daily he was learning to trust God for direction and wisdom. This was a God-sized task and

> Faith in a prayer-hearing God will make a prayer-loving Christian.[1]
> —Andrew Murray

therefore needed God-sized solutions. As the company spent time developing their one hundred-year goal and redefining their position and purpose, the Power family also started growing together again.

Graham spent time with Lauren and his children Gary, Nadene, and Alaine, asking forgiveness for the time when he had been absent in their lives. These acts of repentance between family members gave the Power family the opportunity to reestablish their commitment to each other and to the purposes of God for their individual lives, and also that of the family.

Graham and Lauren started to attend an Alpha Course that was led by their pastor, Dion Forster. Once the Alpha Course was completed, they formed a small cell group that regularly met for Bible study. It was at one of those meetings, only one year after Graham had surrendered his life to the Lord, that Dion announced he had just seen an amazing video, and it was something that he wanted to share with the group. As the large VHS tape was pushed in the machine, there was a feeling of anticipation among the group. What was it that had gotten Dion so excited about the potential for transformation in the city of Cape Town? Without realizing it, Graham and Lauren were sitting and watching the very same tape that Trevor Pearce had brought back from the USA. This was the story that had been circulating among the city prayer groups; this was the *Transformation* video, which told of Cali, Columbia.[2]

Graham's eyes never left the screen. He listened intently to every word, and as he sat absorbed in the story, his heart began to race. He felt a stirring deep within his spirit and started wondering if it was possible in Columbia, then why not Cape Town? There were so many similarities: the gang wars, the poverty, the corruption, the hopelessness of the situation, and a city that was on the way to destruction. The city of Cape Town was gripped in a vice of fear with twenty-two bombs exploding over the previous eighteen months. This documentary ignited a passion deep within his soul, and his newfound trust in God gave him the boldness to believe that what God had done for the people of Cali, Columbia, He could do for the people of South Africa.

Lauren glanced across the room and saw the change in her husband's posture; she saw that familiar look of determination cross his face and the scowl of concentration crease his brow. Without a word being said between the two, she knew that watching this video was a defining moment for Graham. She could see his passion being stirred, and after twenty-one years of marriage she also knew that what they had seen on the TV screen would not remain merely a "good idea," but that Graham would pursue this dream and vision for a transformed South Africa with every fiber of his being.

The responsibilities of CEO continued for Graham, and still he kept asking God for strategies to align his company and family life to biblical principles.

The South African scenario showed little hope of change, and the days moved into weeks. And so it was in June of 2000, with a great sigh of relief, that Graham and Lauren sat on the South Africa Airlines (SAA) flight and headed for Mallorca, Spain. This was a time for the family to regroup and enjoy a four-week holiday together. Lauren knew that this break always refreshed Graham because he left the office and work far behind, and every day spent on the island cruising the balmy waters of the Mediterranean restored him both physically and spiritually.

It had been about six months prior to this that Graham had seen that *Transformation* video, and still the story had not left his mind. Often he would find himself pondering the details. The hope for transformation that had been ignited that night had not dwindled, but Graham had no idea how this could ever become a reality in South Africa. He barely knew the pastors in his own suburb; he was a young Christian and had no credibility in the evangelical community.

As the plane lifted from South African soil, Graham knew that if he were to play any role in the spiritual transformation of South Africa, it would have to be God who led the way and opened doors, because even with all his years of success in business, he had no way of breaking into the unfamiliar world of the church.

How differently Graham began to approach the issues he faced. Even the notion that "God would need to intervene" was a new way of thinking for him. No longer did he feel the need to organize deals and make strategic contacts; God needed to intervene. If these thoughts were from God, then He would need to lead the way. Graham knew that he would be an obedient follower, and with that thought on his mind he fell asleep as the Boeing headed north to sun-kissed beaches and the tropical warm waters of the Mediterranean.

7

THE CYRUS ANOINTING

*Do not store up treasures on earth, where moth and rust
destroy, and where thieves break in and steal. But store up
for yourselves treasures in heaven, where moth and rust do
not destroy, and where thieves do not break in and steal. For
where your treasure is, there your heart will be also.*
—MATTHEW 6:19–21

BACK IN SOUTH Africa after the family time in Spain, Graham walked through the cool interior of the Power Group of Companies head office with a new sense of excitement in his spirit. The winter break had certainly revived his body, but his mind was burning with the details of the clear dream and instructional vision that God had given him only three nights prior to returning home from Mallorca.

He was confident about what God wanted done; now he just needed to know how to go about making the vision a reality. The first step would be to secure the Newlands Stadium for the Day of Repentance and Prayer. This was something that had never happened before, but Graham knew that God was in control of this vision, so he was willing to act in obedience. He determined to contact Rob Wagner, Managing Director of the Western Province Rugby Union, as soon as he got into the office. Graham knew he would need a personal appointment. The request for permission to use the stadium for anything other than rugby was highly irregular, and he imagined it would not be agreed to without some opposition.

Having flown into Cape Town late on Tuesday, Graham drove into the Power offices at exactly 6:00 a.m. ready to attend the morning Bible study. Walking into the meeting room, he was lost in thought and never recognized either of the two women who were already in the meeting.

Later he was to learn that Barbara Cilliers and Annemie Munnik were regular intercessors who were eager to meet him and discuss some insights that they had recently received from the Lord. *The phone call to Rob Wagner will have to wait*, thought Graham as he sat down to attend the Bible study.

Immediately Graham was struck by Barbara's soft smile and gentle spirit; she seemed to have the peace of a person who had spent time in the Lord's presence. Their conversation quickly moved to prayer and to hearing the voice of the Lord. Barbara explained her position as the coordinator for the 24/7 Prayer Watch in the Helderberg Basin. God was calling the church to prayer twenty-four hours, seven days a week. The logistics of organizing these watches were not always that easy, but it was a challenge that was willingly embraced, because Cape Town intercessors firmly believed that this was the time for the awakening of the prayer watchmen over communities and the city.

As Graham listened to their talk about faith and prayer watches, he decided that he would tell the morning group about the vision he had received a few days previously on his annual holiday in Spain. As he recalled the dream, he remembered every detail. He told them about the stadium, the people, the prayers for repentance, the maroon armband with white letters, the goodie bag, and the invitation to the rest of South Africa.

The details just seemed to pour from his mouth. As he spoke, Barbara and Annemie cast a knowing look between themselves, and as they did, both women remembered a prophetic word that had been written down when a group of intercessors had prayed together on the twelfth of August 1998. This prayer meeting had been two years previously.

The heart of the message was that God was going to raise up an instrument of His choice from the Helderberg Basin. This person would affect the nations and would carry the "Cyrus anointing" as described in Isaiah 45.

"Surely this is the man," thought Barbara, and in her heart she rejoiced at God's timing. Before coming to this meeting, Barbara had spent time in prayer. She knew of Graham's reputation as a successful businessman, but on this particular morning she was more concerned about God's heart for the man Graham Power and not just the image of success that the world saw.

While she prayed, she meditated on 1 Kings 7:14–51. It was there she read of King Solomon calling for Huram, the skilled and experienced craftsman. Barbara sensed that God had already prepared Graham Power with the skills of business and the credibility of a man of integrity and success in the community. She believed that God was calling Graham to be a part of building a new temple, a House of Prayer that would have no physical walls but would have an impact that could not be measured by man.

As she recalled the thoughts that the Lord had laid on her heart, and as she listened to the details of the vision given to Graham from God, an indescribable joy stirred. She knew without a doubt that what had just happened in the office was the beginning of the fulfillment of the prophetic promises given to Africa. This was indeed a profound moment; it was the sealing of a promise and the birth of a vision.

The women prayed and left the office. Graham slowly sat down, resting his head on the back of the dark brown leather chair. Then he closed his eyes and quietly prayed for wisdom.

Suddenly he was overwhelmed with a sense of knowledge that the meeting that had just ended was not a chance meeting but was a divine appointment and that God had orchestrated every word of their conversation. He smiled and wondered if this was what it meant to "walk in faith" and to watch God reveal His plans and purposes one step at a time.

Now was the time for the phone call that would secure Newlands Rugby Stadium. Getting the appointment for a few days later, Graham sat and chatted with Rob Wagner. They both lamented over the state of the city. The situation certainly needed some "supernatural intervention." Graham was eager to share the instructional vision that he had received for transformation, and he spoke with passion. Rob Wagner listened to Graham's request, and despite being sympathetic to the urgency of the need, was very deliberate in his words of caution.

This had never been done before; not in one hundred years had Newlands ever been used for anything other than rugby. For South Africans, the rugby turf is hallowed ground, and to set a precedent like this might open other doors in the future.

Despite the words of caution, Graham suggested that they look for a possible date, and together they scanned the 2001 calendar. The date had to be one that did not clash with any other sporting event and was early enough to avoid the winter rains. Suddenly they both saw the most obvious choice. It was Thursday, March 21, 2001. This date was a public holiday for human rights in South Africa.

Graham left the meeting with the tentative support of the managing director and a possible date. He decided that we would also approach the chairman of the board, Mr. Clive Hirschohn, a man of the Jewish faith, and ask him for a favorable consideration to the request for the use of the stadium. Having spoken to these men, and seeing their mutual concern for the state of the city, he wrote the letter of request and submitted it to the Rugby Union Board.

No sooner had he sent the letter than he realized the next board meeting was scheduled for a day after he left South Africa for a tour of Israel. Realizing how important it would be for him to be there, so that he could not only present his case to his colleagues but also respond to any objections that may come, he needed to change his travel plans. He was sure that without his presence there would surely be a delay in the process. Not wanting to waste any time, he had his secretary call all the airlines traveling between South Africa and Israel and tried everything humanly possible to change the date. But every phone call resulted in a negative. There simply were no seats available on any airline. He would have to leave it as scheduled, and he would have to leave the outcome of the letter and the final decision in the hands of God.

> One can believe intellectually in the efficacy of prayer and never do any praying.[3]
> –Catherine Marshall

Boarding the plane was difficult for Graham because every step physically took him out of the range of influence. While he chatted easily to the others on the tour, he kept finding his mind returning to the meeting that would be held the following day.

As the airhostess gave security instructions over the intercom, Graham reluctantly leaned back in his seat, prayed, and asked God to clear the way. He knew that getting the stadium was not just a good idea, it was a God idea, and was crucial to the fulfillment of the vision that God had given him. This was certainly one of the biggest tests of faith that he had yet faced. He had done his part; now God was in control, and it was no longer Graham Power.

The flight was uneventful, and as the plane landed in Israel, passengers were given security clearance allowing for mobile phones to be switched on. Graham turned his phone on, and as he returned the phone to its leather pouch on his belt, he recognized his familiar call tone.

Answering the phone he was surprised to hear the voice of Rob Wagner. He wasted no time in getting to the reason for the call. Rob's voice was filled with excitement and amazement. Quickly he said. "Graham you won't believe it, it's been agreed! It's been approved! You got the stadium."

Turning off the phone, Graham first said a silent prayer of thanks to

God. He was beginning to learn what living by faith and acting in obedience meant, and it was an incredibly humbling experience.

It was at that moment that Graham realized God did not need him to be at the center of every decision made. In fact God did not need Graham Power, but God would use him. He was to be the conduit through which God would move and work. He turned back to the group, and the look of joy on his face was tangible proof of the positive answer he had just received.

In an instant the words of Zechariah 4:6, "'Not by might nor by power, but by my spirit', says the LORD Almighty," became so relevant to this believer who was treading on new ground and blazing a way where others had not been before.

While the days of traveling in Israel and discovering significant places of importance for the Christian church were meaningful, Graham could not wait to get home so that preparations for the prayer meeting he had seen in the vision could begin in earnest.

Still he was not sure how he would mobilize the church in the city of Cape Town, but Graham was on a mission with God, and nothing or no one was going to stop his progress. The flight home seemed to take an eternity as Graham, a mover and shaker in the business world, was ready to ignite the same passion in the Christian community.

Little did he know or imagine what lay ahead. The path was not an easy road; there were many obstacles in the way. Graham Power would soon be surprised and even disappointed at the amount of politics and resistance to a move of God among the city pastors.

8
BREAKTHROUGH

*"Love the Lord your God with all your heart and with all your soul
and with all your mind." This is the first and greatest command-
ment. And the second is like it: "Love your neighbor as yourself."*
—MATTHEW 22:37–39

WITH THE APPROVAL from the Rugby Union, and the dedication
of a man determined to make every detail of the vision a reality,
Graham began to reschedule his diary and to spend time meeting
with Christian leaders in both the church and business. Then to his
complete surprise, a barrage of opposition came from the most unlikely
source—the church.

There were still a number of legalities that needed to be processed
in regard to the use of Newlands Stadium, but a slow and systematic
approach to these issues soon dispensed of all objections. Handling these
objections seemed easier to manage than all the conflict between denominations and churches. It was not as easy to break down the walls of
suspicion and mistrust among the various denominational and pastoral
fraternals. The body of Christ in the city of Cape Town was a broken and
hurting body; getting them to agree to pray together felt like a bigger
hurdle than getting the approval for the use of the stadium.

Graham felt as if he were on a personal mission. He began to search
for opportunities to speak to the church leaders in Cape Town. These
opportunities were neither easy to come by, nor very welcoming. Graham
had several things against him. Firstly, Graham Power was an unknown
name in Christian circles. Questions began to circulate. Who was he?
Which church did he attend? How long had he been a Christian? Was
this a charismatic or a conservative meeting? Whose banner would this
meeting be held under? Whose authority and covering did he have?

At this time CTCT members and other Christian leaders began to
gather around Graham. Each one had a unified desire to see the transformation of their city. With this as their motivation, they formed the
Transformation Africa committee. Together they were going to plan the

prayer day and invite the churches of Cape Town to join together for prayer.

Numerous meetings had been scheduled, but the response had been slow and not very encouraging. Standing and sharing his vision with a particular group of pastors in the city, Graham once again felt the resistance and quietly prayed for a breakthrough. Surely this could not be the state of the church? He felt very uneasy as he realized that despite having been in a cutthroat business for many years, nothing had prepared him for the conflict that he was facing in the body of Christ. He soon realized that many of the same attitudes that presided in the business world were present in the church. The only difference was that the church had acquired a few more seemingly sanctified names for their attitudes.

It had been a long morning for Graham with several business meetings and then the meeting with a group of spiritual leaders and pastors in an area of Cape Town called Langa. He was going to tell them about God's vision for the city. He was still desperately trying to get support from the leadership. With time slipping away, he was beginning to doubt whether it was even a vague possibility that the church could put aside its differences, support the vision, and actually gather for a time of repentance and prayer.

Langa is an area on the outskirts of Cape Town that had been created during the apartheid years, when white communities wanted to move black families away from the center of commerce and good residential areas. *Langa* is a Xhosa word meaning "sun,"[1] but the hardship of living in this impoverished, overcrowded area had not left place for much sunshine to warm the lives of the thousands of people who were its residents.

Power Construction had developed many of the roads in the Western Cape, so Graham was familiar with many of the back routes. The narrow roads, lined with shacks or small informal dwellings, were not easy to navigate. Small children played in the road, as this was their only playground. Unemployed young men sat on empty beer crates, mindlessly puffing on short cigarettes while thin dogs sniffed through the litter that covered the streets.

As he drove to the pastors' meeting, Graham prayed that God would give him the courage to present the vision, walk humbly and not harden his heart, and believe that today he would see the power of God at work in the lives of community pastors and leaders.

Once again he stood in front of the group and spoke of the vision to unite the city in prayer and then invite the rest of South Africa to join together to pray for the transformation of the nation. No sooner had he finished sharing his story than he began receiving quick and vehement opposition. Concerns over insufficient time, logistics, and planning came quickly, with little reprise.

Standing aside, Graham let a friend and member of the Transformation Africa committee, Trevor Goddard, answer many of the questions. Trevor Goddard was another sporting hero in South Africa. Once acclaimed for his all-around performance on the cricket pitch, he had captained the South African team to victory on many occasions. Since his retirement from cricket, Trevor Goddard had become an itinerant evangelist. On this occasion he carried no national colors but just a love for his nation and a desire to see lives changed for Christ.

As he successfully fielded one question after the other, he added that the concerns about timing were really irrelevant, because Graham Power's company could just as easily build a stadium within the time frame of six months, than to simply fill it with people.

Believing in the African concept of *ubuntu*, which is an African expression used to encourage unity and consensus in decision-making, Graham let the discussion continue much longer than he would have in the constraints of his boardroom, which was governed by the clock and directed by his leadership. The room got hotter, and for a moment his mind wandered away from the debate until he was sharply brought back to the moment by a voice that broke through the questioning crowd.

Slowly standing to her feet, a woman called Mamela spoke with conviction and authority. The room seemed to settle in an instant as her voice cried out, "What is this thing? When God gives a vision, we are not to question, we are to come alongside and support."

Silence followed. And in those moments of silence, it seemed as though a door had been unlocked in the heavenlies. Was this the moment that Graham and the Transformation Africa committee had been waiting for? It only lasted a few seconds, but it could be said that while God had conceived the vision in the heart of Graham Power in Spain, this moment marked the beginning of the labor pains. Could the vision finally become a reality in the hearts of the people of Cape Town?

The first man to courageously stand to his feet was Reverend Willem Malherbe. It had only been a week before that Willem had attended a presentation as a member of the Dutch Reformed Fraternity in Durbanville.

This fraternity had initially expressed strong reservations against the idea of a united day of prayer. Willem stood tall among the crowd, and with a voice that lilted with his Afrikaans accent humbly said, "I want to support Mamela. I do now believe that this is a vision from God, and I want to support it."

As he sat down, he too had a sense that this was a significant moment for the church in Cape Town, but never could he have imagined the impact that this day would have as a catalyst in the global story of transformation and prayer. One by one, other leaders started to nod, and then as the Holy Spirit sealed the issue in their hearts, they too stood to their feet and voiced their approval and agreed to stand in unity.

Graham drove back to the office along the same route as he had driven earlier that day. As he drove, the same children still played in the street, the same young men sat on the empty beer boxes, and even the same dogs sniffed through the garbage, but this time Graham was not the same. The heaviness had lifted. He felt the excitement of anticipation and expectation. As he drove along the familiar streets his heart cried out, "Hallelujah! The first victory has finally been won."

Mamela died shortly after the second Transformation Prayer day. She may never have fully understood how significant her voice was in breaking the bondage of disunity and unbelief. There was, however, little doubt in the minds of those who attended that meeting that the boldness of Mamela was used by God to promote prayer and unity in the city.

All around Cape Town, men and women were turning their hearts to God and begging Him to intervene in the critical political and social issues facing the city. Despite the urgency of the needs, there was not always unity or conformity within the body of Christ. It is for this very reason that men and women who receive a word of instruction from the Lord need to persevere and determine that nothing or no one will stop them from being obedient.

News about this proposed day of repentance and prayer was beginning to circulate in the Christian community, and Barbara Cilliers was eager to introduce Graham Power to Dr. Bennie Mostert, who was the founder and coordinator of Jericho Walls. An opportune moment presented itself when Bennie was the guest speaker at a prayer gathering. No sooner was the meeting over than the two men shook hands and stood face to face in the restaurant.

Barbara, knowing the continual time pressures on Graham's schedule, asked him to tell Bennie about the vision for a Day of Repentance and Prayer. Bennie stood and listened to Graham recall the details of the vision, and finally the instruction to hire the stadium and then to invite all of Africa to join together in prayer. Bennie is known to be a man of few words, and once again on this occasion his words were direct and to the point. He very quietly expressed his doubts that the church would be able to come together and then suggested that Graham reconsider the timing of this event.

Once again Graham was facing the same questions and the same degree of doubt, but this time he never experienced any doubt in his own mind. He knew that he was going to be obedient to God and that he would follow every detail of the instruction. No matter the thoughts and ideas of Christian leaders, he would trust God to make this day a reality.

In the months and years to come, Bennie Mostert reconsidered his opinion. Today he is an active participator and advocate for the Global Day of Prayer and is being used by God in the growth of the 24/7 prayer initiatives throughout Africa.

As prayer for Cape Town and South Africa began to intensify, Sharing of Ministries Abroad (SOMA) planned to have a four-day consultation on transformation in Cape Town. Guest speakers included George Otis, Harold Caballeros, Ruth Ruebal, Emeka Nwankpa, and Alister Petrie.

Following the consultation, Community Transformation graciously agreed to host the international speakers and invited them to address a gathering of leaders at a national conference on transformation that was held at Lighthouse Church. The conference reached a climax when delegates were invited to join a city-wide prayer meeting on November 5, 2000.

And then the miracle happened; the breakthrough the praying Christians had been waiting for finally came. An unexploded pipe bomb was discovered only a few kilometers away from Lighthouse Church, and then later that very day the men who had planted the bomb were arrested and put in custody.

God had heard the cries of his people. Today it is a documented fact that since the discovery of that unexploded bomb there has not been another explosion in the city of Cape Town. Prayer was making a difference.

The following day the city newspapers carried this headline: "Breakthrough."

Graham had been invited to attend and was eager to go because he wanted to talk to the people who had been involved in the transformation of Cali, Columbia. Memories of watching the video filled his mind, and he wanted to know the hearts of the people; he wanted to hear how God had used ordinary people to change an entire community. This would be his opportunity to meet with the Sentinel Group and George Otis, Jr. As the CTCT (Cape Town Community Transformation) conference ended, every delegate left with a copy of the *Transformation* video.

Now was the time to share God's vision. Together with the assistance of prominent city pastors and leaders, Trevor Pearce, Eddie Edson, Willem Malherbe, and Mike Winfield, Graham invited one hundred local Christian leaders and most of the international guests to a cocktail party at the President's Suite in the Newlands Stadium.

As men and women mingled, encouraging one another with stories of answered prayer, Graham followed George Otis outside onto the balcony and had a quiet conversation that would in the months to come serve as a motivator not to give up the fight for unity and prayer in the city.

Standing alone, looking out over an empty stadium, often creates a feeling of melancholy. The reality of being one person in the middle of a space that has the capacity for thousands seems to highlight our need for interdependence and unity. The wind was blowing through the empty stadium as the two men stood on the balcony and looked out over the sea of blue seats. Graham took the time to explain every detail of the vision God had given him. Together they shared a passion and a desire to see every seat filled with people from every denomination and race standing before God in prayer. Trying to generate the same degree of passion in a divided church had been difficult for Graham, and tonight standing outside, he admitted his feelings of disappointment to George Otis.

Listening to both the words and emotions contained in Graham's voice, George finally spoke. "Graham," he said quietly," I have been in Cape Town for more than a week and have spoken to many spiritual and business leaders, and I want to tell you that there is so much disunity in your city, there is so much negativity, that I wonder whether God even feels welcome in your city."

These words cut to the core. Surely it could not be the truth. This simple statement motivated Graham to study God's Word with renewed intensity. He was determined to discover what God said about unity in the body of Christ. Within days the words of Ephesians 4:3–6 became the central theme of Graham's messages:

> Make every effort to keep the unity of the Spirit through the bond of peace. There is one body and one Spirit—just as you were called to one hope when you were called—one Lord, one faith, one baptism; one God and Father of all, who is over all and through all and in all.

As this theme of unity began to take hold of the leaders, they began to show that with God it was possible to put aside the differences that divide and to find common ground in the Lord Jesus Christ.

The overseas team returned home, and the Cape Town team continued to plan the details for the day of prayer. The first pastors' meeting was held at Newlands in January 2001, and to the surprise of all, three hundred fifty pastors and spiritual leaders arrived. As they stood outside in the hot sun and joined hands in prayer, trusting God that every seat would be filled, they spoke with one voice and trusted with one heart. Graham believed that God was beginning to feel a warm invitation of welcome from the body of Christ in the city of Cape Town.

The second meeting, only one month later, was even more surprising when six hundred seventy pastors arrived. Once again they prayed for unity and for a stadium filled to overflowing with Christians from every denomination and walk of life. The request for tickets had reached an unprecedented seventy thousand. As the stadium could only accommodate forty-five thousand, careful planning and administration were required to ensure that crowd control was well maintained.

As the planning continued, so did the prayer. It is estimated that for twenty-one days preceding the first Transformation Africa Day of Prayer more than three hundred churches prayed 24/7 for this event. And while groups of people spent days in prayer and fasting for the event, men such as Mike Winfield carefully coordinated the prayer guideline for the Day of Prayer. Every aspect of the program, every item that would be prayed for, was carefully thought about and prayed for. Mike was determined to make the day a day that was driven by God's agenda and not the good ideas of men.

While much of the prayer was for transformation, unity, and even for the salvation of people attending, many hours were spent in urgent prayer, waiting for the final letter of approval for the use of the stadium.

The Uni-City of Cape Town still had not presented the letter of approval to use the stadium for an event that was not sports related. Some of their concerns included the noise level in the community, and the city needed to ensure that there were no dissenting voices from the residents. In fact the law said that even three negative votes from the ratepayers association could result in a withdrawal of the license.

The good news was that both the premier, Mr. Gerald Morkel, and the Cape Town City mayor, Mr. Peter Marais, had attended the February leaders meeting at Newlands and were standing behind the request to use the stadium; but still the stark reality remained that without this letter of approval the prayer day could be cancelled, even at this late stage. The entire committee was anxiously waiting to hear that approval had been received. The weeks became days and still they heard nothing, and then finally with only hours to go, Graham received the final letter of approval from the city of Cape Town. The way was clear to hold the first Transformation Africa Day of Prayer in Newlands.

9
THE DREAM BECOMES A REALITY

You intended to harm me, but God intended it for good to accomplish what is now being done, the saving of many lives.
—GENESIS 50:20

AT EXACTLY 3:00 a.m. on March 21, 2001, Graham awoke restless, tossing in bed and wondering if he had done all that was required of him. In a whisper that was barely audible he prayed, "Father, have I been completely obedient, and will this prayer offering be pleasing to You?" With less than twelve hours to go before the start of the Day of Prayer, it was impossible to go back to sleep, so he decided that rather than just waiting for the time to pass, he would spend time in prayer. Quietly slipping out of bed, he walked down the dark passage into his study where for several hours he waited on the Lord and trusted God for a miracle.

This first Day of Repentance and Prayer was also a public holiday in South Africa. It was Human Rights Day, the day that the nation remembered the Sharpeville massacre where in 1960 sixty-nine people where shot and killed by South African police as they staged a protest against the discriminatory Pass Law. This law stated that all black people were required to carry a "pass-book" that contained their fingerprints, photograph, and information on their access into white areas. It was only after the democratic elections of 1994 that the twenty-first of March was set aside as a day when the nation declared that such a violation of human rights would never happen again.

While the Christians were preparing to meet for repentance and prayer in Newlands Stadium, the African National Congress (ANC), the governing party, were planning political remembrance meetings across the nation.

Throughout the night, Barbara and her team held a prayer vigil, committing every detail to the Lord. The Cape Town office, manned by Low Bothma and Antinia De Waal, had prayed and planned for every detail of this day. They had done their part and were now just waiting for the hours to pass so the city of Cape Town could gather for repentance and prayer.

From early in the morning, sound engineers set about erecting their equipment. Young men and women packed the small plastic bags with a fruit juice, a prayer card, burgundy armbands with white embroidery, and a small snack. Each bag also included the booklet *Four Spiritual Laws*.

Helpers and volunteers then watched as the trucks filled with prayer cards and bags began to arrive at the stadium. Together they formed a human chain as the boxes were passed from the trucks to every entrance into the stadium. Small groups of prayer warriors gathered in every corner of Newlands and slowly walked up and down the rows of empty seats, praying and trusting God for the people who would soon occupy every place in the stadium. Their words were lost in the great empty space, but God the Father heard their prayers as they prepared the spiritual climate for the forty-five thousand people who would soon enter the stadium. Young dancers went through their paces on the green grass, and still the requests for more tickets kept coming.

The impossible had happened; for the first time in the history of the church in Cape Town, the body of Christ was gathering for prayer and worship in such large numbers. There were no famous names on the program, there was no band with a following, there was just a desire to plead with God for the city and the nation.

As the stadium preparations continued, one hundred buses moved into the surrounding townships and communities. In some areas the buses arrived to find long lines of men and women already waiting. Despite holding a travel voucher in their hands, they had arrived an hour or two earlier than expected so they could be guaranteed a place on the bus and in the stadium. Event organizers had contracted for ten designated trains, each able to transport 1,250 people, to run along both of the city's railroad lines. This was a gathering of God's children, and everyone was invited.

The atmosphere was electric. Spontaneously, strangers turned to one another and started praying. They joined hands and asked God to bless every aspect of the day. Ordinary people broke into song, and carriages filled with sounds of rejoicing moved through the suburbs of Cape Town, all heading for their final destination, Newlands Stadium.

Children sat wide-eyed, clapping and dancing to the rhythm of the worship songs. There was no class designation on these trains and buses, just a gathering of God's people to meet for prayer and worship.

As the train doors opened, hundreds of believers spilled onto the platforms and quickly moved into the stadium. The metal turnstile gates kept spinning, and with every rotation another person entered into the sport ground, playing their part in making history. As the crowd continued to gather in the stadium, families, prison inmates, pensioners, and friends gathered to listen to the live radio broadcast that would carry the events of the day far beyond the gates of the stadium. In order to accommodate the request for seats, several churches opened their doors and used closed-circuit satellite feeds to join in this day of unity and prayer.

The program was led by Christian leaders from every denomination and cultural group. The theme for the day was repentance and prayer, and every speaker directed the crowd back to the saving grace of the Lord Jesus Christ. One speaker clearly stated that the first step in preparing for revival was personal repentance and then corporate repentance for the sins of our nation.

As believers took hands with Christians from across the cultural, economic, and racial divide, healing began to happen. Men and women wept uncontrollably for the pain caused by the greatest curse on their land—apartheid. Prayer leaders gave the crowd the opportunity to turn to one another and to present the needs of their neighbors to the throne of grace and mercy. The main issues that were prayed for on this day included crime and violence, gangsterism, substance abuse, HIV/AIDS, families, unemployment, and a break in the drought that had plagued the region for months. As each prayer item came to an end, there was an overwhelming cry for spiritual revival and transformation in the city and the nation.

> Who has ever heard of such a thing? Who has ever seen such things? Can a country be born in a day or a nation be brought forth in a moment?
> —Isaiah 66:8

News about this event, and the subjects that were being prayed for, soon came to the attention of the media, who like moths to a flame descended on the presidential suite at Newlands. Journalists and news reporters kept asking the prayer coordinators what had precipitated this unusual gathering of forty-five thousand people. Their answer was a unanimous statement of faith and confidence in the fact that only God is able to change the situation in their nation, and that He promised that if His people who are called by His name would humble themselves, repent, seek His face, and turn from their wicked ways then He would hear from heaven, forgive their sin, and heal their land. (See 2 Chronicles 7:14.)

This was the Christian church in the city of Cape Town acting in obedience and asking God to heal their land.

As the Church of England bishop, Frank Retief, closed the meeting with the words of the benediction, the youth band started playing "Jabulani," a song of joy from the people of Africa. As the words of praise, worship, and celebration echoed around the stadium, forty-five thousand people quickly cleared the seats. And as they left, they were encouraged to take their papers and garbage with them. By the time the stadium was empty, it was litter free. This was a small but significant thank offering to the organizers and the stadium managers for the gratitude of being able to use this venue.

Heading back to their respective buses and trains, men, women, and children walked hand in hand, singing and rejoicing. As the train conductors blew their final whistles and the last train departed from Newlands station, there was such an overwhelming sense of satisfaction, knowing that this was not the end, but just the beginning of something great, something beyond their wildest dreams and imaginations.

While the people headed home in the setting sun, a storm was brewing in the Presidential Suite at Newlands. At about 4:00 p.m., while the prayers continued in the stadium, Graham Power had made his way to the Presidential Suite where he was going to meet with friends and thank the Lord for the incredible day that was about to come to an end. No sooner had he entered than a reporter and a news camera crew cornered him with the question, "Mr. Power, what is your response to the attack from the political arena?"

Caught totally off-guard, Graham was confused. Questions raced through his mind, "What attack? Which political arena?" He needed more information. It was soon very obvious to the media crew that Graham was oblivious to the accusations that were being made about this gathering by one of the political leaders in the city. Quickly and with the succinctness of an experienced news team, the reporter filled Graham in on the details.

Only ten kilometers away in a venue that could hold thousands, a Human Rights Day remembrance service had been planned by the government.

To the surprise of the organizers, this event was poorly attended. The contrast between the forty-five thousand people in Newlands and the several hundred in Athlone was at the bottom of the verbal attack. The Minister of Education, Kadar Asmal, saw this as an intentional attempt to bring about division and to entrench the mindset of separateness. *The Cape Times*, a local newspaper, carried the headline "50,000 Christians Pack Newlands—Asmal Slams 'Sectarian' Rally. "

The article read, "Education Minister Kadar Asmal launched an attack on the 'divisive' mass Christian rally at Fedsure Park Newlands Rugby Stadium yesterday attended by more than fifty thousand people." Asmal said the mass meeting constituted the gathering of a "sectarian body" responsible for enhancing divisions in South Africa.[1]

While nothing could have been further from the truth, all the main TV stations and news broadcasters led with that story in the evening news. Many people who had been at the Repentance and Prayer Day returned home with a hope and joy in their hearts and eagerly turned on their televisions expecting to see this story of "good news" being broadcast across the nation. But there was no good news, just the report that in Cape Town, Minister Asmal attacked Christians. The visual images, used as cutaways for the news, briefly showed the crowded stadium, but then gave a disproportionate amount of time to the poorly attended Human Rights Day service.

Within hours the media saw the potential for a story that would catch the attention of politicians and Christians alike. Graham Power was soon inundated with phone calls, requests for interviews, and comments from both secular and Christian radio stations. Over the next three days every major newspaper in the nation carried this event as a front-page story. Numerous debates were had in the editorial columns, letters were written to the editors, and while the furor continued, the success of the first day of repentance and prayer was being told across the nation.

At first despondent and discouraged by the verbal attack, Graham was quick to see how God was using the media to spread the story. This event had received far more coverage than could have been given in one evening news broadcast. There was no doubt in his mind that what Satan had intended for evil, God was turning to good.

As the media debate continued, the Transformation Africa Committee received hundreds of calls of support, encouragement, and promises of prayer from churches and businessmen around the country.

Despite the words of encouragement, Graham knew that he needed to go and personally see the man who had made the verbal attack, Minister Kadar Asmal. This would be a sensitive meeting and needed much wisdom. Hundreds of Christians started praying for this meeting, and Graham begged the Lord for compassion and understanding.

About three weeks later a meeting was arranged for a Wednesday morning, and after much prayer Graham and two other Transformation Africa committee members arrived at the offices of the Minister of Education. The goal of this meeting was to communicate the heart of the day, and to explain that this event was not aimed at causing division but unity, and that the Christian community was crying out for peace in the city. The small delegation also took a recorded video, which had been produced by Media Village, showing excerpts from the Day of Prayer.

After the formal greetings were over, the VHS tape was pushed into the video machine; and crucial moments of prayer for the needs of the nation, the prayers for leaders in government and authority, the cries of repentance for the atrocity of apartheid, and the call for unity in our beloved South Africa filled the room. There was no mistaking the intention of the Transformation Africa Prayer Day. Camera pans across the capacity-packed stadium showed Mr. Asmal that it was filled with men, women, and children from every race and culture. This was not only a true reflection of the body of Christ but also of the people of South Africa. Suddenly words such as *divisive* and *sectarian* that had been used to describe this meeting lost their power.

A few days later, a letter was published in *The Cape Argus* from Professor Kadar Asmal, in which he said, "I do wish to express regret to the many thousands of Christians, including, no doubt, members of the ANC, who turned up at the Newlands event and also to others who were hurt by some of my comments in the speech that I made. I fully accept the bona fides of those who gathered on Human Rights Day, and I fully accept the right of Christians, as such, as well as of particular churches to assemble together."[3]

This letter in the editorial section of the newspaper once again kindled interest in the media, and the debate continued for several more days. Graham felt that it was important to respond to the minister's letter of apology, and he received a front-page citation saying, "It is regrettable that Professor Asmal expressed his personal feelings while addressing a large gathering of people, but at the end of the day, he did apologize for his utterances."³

The small group of men who had gone to the minister's office had gone in peace, seeking reconciliation. The printed letter through the media was evidence that they had truly reaped what they had sown and that God had used the entire week to catapult the attention of the country toward the power of prayer.

No sooner had the public attention begun to die away than the Transformation Africa committee began to receive testimonies from people who had either attended or listened to the prayer day on the radio.

Heideveld is a poor suburb of Cape Town and is often plagued with crime and gang activity, but a pastor from this community told an amazing story of his experience directly after the prayer day. He was sitting at home when the doorbell rang, and standing outside was a young man. He seemed nervous, and there was a rough edge to his mannerisms. He steadied himself by holding onto the doorframe, and as his hand reached out, the pastor saw the maroon Transformation Africa armband. Before he could ask any questions, the man started speaking. He seemed to stumble over his words, but he was determined to keep talking. He said, "Pastor, I have to see you. I was there by Newlands yesterday. I committed my life to Jesus Christ, and now I want to confess my sin and ask for your forgiveness. A few years ago when I was a thief and a criminal, I broke into your house and stole your television, Hi-Fi, and some other things. It was worth a lot of money. I want to apologize to you. I am sorry, and if you want to take me to the police station I will come with you right now."

The pastor reached out and touched his arm, and then taking his hand into his own said, "What you have done today is good, but I forgave you years ago; and now that you have become a son of God, you are part of our family. I want you to come to church on Sunday and tell the entire congregation this good news about Jesus who has saved you."

At Pollsmoor Prison, where Nelson Mandela had once been incarcerated, a warden told the story to the inmates of a friend who had driven through a dangerous part of town late at night. His car had broken down, and while he sat there waiting for help to come, he heard the windows being shattered as four young men broke into his car and began to attack him. They stole his wallet, watch, and phone, and hit him across the face. He began to lose consciousness, and in the distance he heard one of his attackers discussing the fact that he was wearing the Transformation Africa armband, and was probably a Christian.

Deciding against killing a "holy man," they took their plunder and left the man for dead on the side of the road. As the victim began to realize his situation, he tried to stop oncoming vehicles. He was covered in blood, and in the midst of a society governed by fear, people thought this may be a trap, and no one was willing to stop and give assistance. Finally, a passing vehicle filled with passengers who were returning from a church meeting noticed that the man who was so desperately trying to get help was wearing the Transformation Africa armband. They decided to stop and rescue him.

Once in the vehicle, the driver was quick to tell the injured man that had he not seen the armband he would never have had the courage to stop. He had felt prompted by God, knowing that only days prior they had prayed together for the transformation of the city.

Every action of kindness, every deed of compassion, and every day that passed without a bomb exploding was evidence that God was at work in the city of Cape Town, South Africa. While all these stories were beginning to unfold across the city, Media Village was gathering the footage from the cameras around the stadium. Media Village is a ministry of Youth With A Mission, and several years prior to the first Day of Prayer the founders Graham and Diane Vermooten had committed their ministry to not only training but also to telling the stories of God around the globe.

As their team worked through the night editing the footage, they could never have dreamed or imagined that their DVDs and stories would carry the story of Transformation Africa and then later the Global Day of Prayer around the world.

Graham Power was later to say that although there was no doubt of the fact that Transformation Africa and the Global Day of Prayer was a move of God, it was spurred on by the powerful visual images and the stories produced by Media Village.

10

A GROWING TEAM

I will make you into a great nation and I will bless you; I will make your name great, and you will be a blessing. I will bless those who bless you, and whoever curses you I will curse; and all peoples on earth will be blessed through you.

—Genesis 12:2–3

THE TRANSFORMATION AFRICA committee wasted no time in evaluating the first Day of Prayer, and together they asked for new strategies that would enable them to fulfill the second part of the instruction given to Graham by God. It was time to invite South Africa to join together for repentance and prayer. After a few formalities and legalities, Newlands Fedsure Stadium was once again secured. This date was March 21, 2002, and eight other cities were invited to be a part of the day of prayer.

Frans Cronje, a member of the committee, who had been actively involved in mobilizing the youth to help with the logistics of the first prayer day, firmly believed that the youth would play an important role in the growth of this movement. Frans headed up a youth sports ministry called Sport for Christ Action South Africa (SCAS) and was always on the lookout for meaningful mission opportunities for the young sports people. In June 2001, just a few months after the Newlands Day of Prayer, Frans believed that God gave him a vision to mobilize Christians to run across the country carrying a message of hope through salvation to be found in the person of Jesus Christ. The run would be called "The Walk of Hope." Not only would this walk encourage people on the highways and byways of the country, but it would also serve to be an important tool in raising the awareness of this significant day. It was decided that as the city of Bloemfontein is at the heart of the nation, teams would all depart from that city and then move toward the eight stadia where a Transformation Africa Prayer Day would be held in 2002.

Graham Power looked back at the effect of the first day of prayer, at the reconciliation with Professor Asmal, at the specific answers to prayer, and knew that his life would never be the same. The full impact of his collision with God's destiny and purpose for his life was yet to be experienced, but he was determined to live out every day in humble obedience and take every opportunity given to him. Sharing the vision and inviting others to join were just some of the ways that Graham actively pursued the fulfillment of the vision. Sitting in committee and planning meetings, and listening to the idea for a national Walk of Hope, all inspired the visionary thinker, but deep in his heart Graham knew that God still needed to provide a national strategy and the people who could take the vision to make it a reality. Quietly he prayed, not even sure for whom or what he was asking. Graham was still the CEO of the Power Group, and his business workload had not diminished in the slightest. God would need to provide a team who were not only passionate but also able to manage and grow the vision to its capacity.

In February 2002, Graham accepted an invitation to speak at the largest Dutch Reformed Church in the nation, Morelleta Park DRC. The leaders of this church had already been exposed to prayer organizations such as Jericho Walls and the Network of United Prayer in South Africa (NUPSA). Men such as Dr. Bennie Mostert had actively engaged the church in prayer initiatives, and the 24/7 prayer movement was beginning to grow in the region. God was moving in the nation, and this church was on a mission with God, determined to play its role in mobilizing its members to prayer for nation transformation.

> I have so much to do that I spend several hours in prayer before I am able to do it.[1]
> –John Wesley

Dawie and Isebel Spangenberg attended Moreleta Park and were faithful members of a cell group, actively participating in the life of the church. Dawie had, like Graham Power, also received the Businessman of the Year award. These two men both had a passion for sports and business, and over the years their paths had crossed in these two arenas on various occasions. As the tyranny of the urgent invaded both their lives, they had lost contact for several years; but when Dawie heard the church announcement stating that Graham Power would be the guest speaker at a service in a few weeks, he determined that he would rekindle the friendship. Dawie offered to pick Graham up from the airport and host him in his home on the night of the speaking engagement.

Dawie and Isebel were desperately seeking the will of God for their lives. Like the successful Graham, they too had a game farm, a beautiful home, the latest cars, and the recognition of the business world. As CEO and owner of the second largest security company in the nation, the Spangenbergs lived an extremely busy but satisfied and comfortable life. But all those securities were suddenly in the balance as Dawie had to face one of the most difficult decisions of his life. He had discovered unethical practices were being conducted in his company, and he had a choice to make: be part of the cover-up or expose the wrongdoing. The decision to expose what was going on would have major ramifications not only for his family and company, but also for some of the major financial institutions in the nation.

As they drove to the airport to pick up Graham, Dawie knew that he would be able to chat with his old friend and that he would understand the dilemma that he faced. Like many South Africans, Dawie had followed the story of Graham's conversion, and he was eager to hear his story. Parking the car, both Dawie and Isebel entered the airport to pick up Graham Power, but neither of them could have ever dreamed or imagined the significance of that meeting. Talk was easy for the two friends; they quickly filled the gap made by the passing years and then prepared for church.

Graham stood behind the podium and told the story of his life. He spoke with a new gentle but bold confidence; he spoke of the pleasant allure of success and wealth but the emptiness that comes when every material goal is attained. He told of his vision, how God had turned his life upside down, of the repositioning of his company, and of the first Transformation Africa Prayer Day in Newlands. He showed the video, and any doubts in the minds of the listeners were removed, as people saw a stadium filled with people, not cheering at the scoring of a goal but rejoicing and worshiping before the King of kings.

The audience was captivated and motivated to play their role in the Transformation Prayer movement in South Africa. As Dawie and Isebel sat in the church, God began to stir their hearts. Graham spoke for his allocated time, but it seemed as though the presentation was over within minutes of starting. Graham was inundated with questions, and while he stood and answered them, the Spangenbergs quietly slipped out of the church and waited in the vehicle for Graham to join them.

Sitting in the dark, Isebel finally spoke the words that had burned on her heart all night. Tossing her blonde hair from her shoulder, she leaned forward and said, "So did you hear what God said to you tonight?" Hearing the voice of God was new territory for Dawie, and he responded with a quick, "No, but what do you think God said to me tonight?"

It seemed such a perfect fit, with both Graham and Dawie sharing similar backgrounds. Graham talked of filling stadiums, and Dawie knew how to obtain, manage, and prepare them for major events. They were both men who had tasted success, but at the crossroads of their lives both wanted significance—God's significance.

The conversation just seemed to hang in the darkness, and Isebel kept asking her husband to "just talk to Graham," a request that Dawie did not totally agree to. Quietly they continued to sit in the dark car waiting for Graham Power to join them.

Graham's flight was at 6:00 a.m. the following morning, so it was an early rising for both men. As they drove to the airport, Dawie could hear Isebel's words from the night before, "just talk to him," echo in the car.

He never said a word. Small talk was the subject, and verbal agreements to stay in touch guaranteed that the trip soon came to an end. As Graham grabbed his overnight bag from the backseat he reached out and shook Dawie's hand and thanked him for the hospitality, but Dawie knew this was not the time for greetings. This was the time to make an offer. Still uncertain about what the offer meant, Dawie told Graham that he had some time available and would be willing to assist the team planning the Walk of Hope.

"Are you sure?" Graham quickly responded. Knowing Dawie's experience and skills, he was eager to continue the conversation, but there was no time to continue, as the boarding announcement for the flight back to Cape Town would happen in a few minutes.

"I have a few weeks, so let's see what I can do," was the calm and collected response from Dawie.

"I'll call you as soon as I get back to Cape Town," said Graham. With these words as the parting salutation, the men who had just renewed their friendship once again went their separate ways. This time, however, they were both following God's agenda, and their lives would soon be intricately linked in the desire to bring about God's vision for Africa.

Back at the Power head office in Cape Town, Graham wasted no time in phoning Dawie. By the end of that phone call, Dawie had committed to assisting with the Walk of Hope. This call marked the beginning of a journey together, the course of which would cross the globe and unite believers from every corner of the world.

With military precision that was an automatic response from Dawie, he contacted Frans Cronje and decided that the only way to ensure buy-in from the towns and cities on the Walk of Hope route would be to personally visit, inspire, and motivate the Christian leaders from every city. The easiest source of information was a pastor's list of the Dutch Reformed Church and Apostolic Faith Mission (AFM) churches. Dawie and Isebel left their two young children with her parents and headed down to the city of Bloemfontein.

The plan was confirmed. Each city on route would send a group of runners to the previous town. They would pick up the message scroll and relay baton and would then run directly to their own hometown. On arrival the mayor or spiritual leaders would read the previous messages and add their own words of encouragement for the next city. Each team would then arrive at the eight stadia around the nation on the Day of Prayer, bringing messages of hope and encouragement. The goal was to cover a total of 4,400 kilometers run by 770 runners who together would visit sixty-five towns and cities.

Dawie studied the road map and soon determined the route that the team who would run to Ellis Park Stadium in Johannesburg would need to follow. Getting into their car, they traveled to every town, made a phone call to the local pastor, asked for an appointment, and then made the presentation. In some towns they were welcomed with open arms, and pastors promised full participation and support. This was, however, not the case in every town; in fact, some places even ushered them out of their area and told them not to speak to their congregations about unity. Dawie was later to tell Graham how shocked and surprised he was at the condition of the church. In most cities the body of Christ was not a reflection of God's heart for unity. There were few cities in the entire region that even had a pastor's fraternal.

Driving home, Dawie began to feel the immensity of the task at hand. Even the best strategies and man-made plans needed God to intervene and to bring about unity in the hearts of His children. This was not just a problem faced by churches of different races but also denominations. If the Walk of Hope was going to be successful, local churches would have to put aside their differences and start working together, and if they did,

the power of unity had the potential to turn this one event into the catalyst for change throughout the nation.

Praying for Africa in Cape Town, South Africa

Symbolically praying for the nations of the world

The armband that reminded
thousands of their commitment
to pray

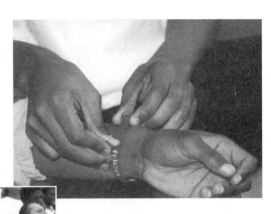

Graham Power leading Newlands
Stadium in repentance and prayer

100,000 gathered to pray in Jakarta, Indonesia

The prayer meeting that started the 10 days of prayer and fasting in 2005

Young and old gather to worship

Young people completing the Walk of Hope

Surrender and worship

The t-shirts that motivated youth to keep praying for Africa

Thousands gather in the Cave Church in Garbage City, Egypt

11
THE VISION EMBRACES THE WORLD

*But you will receive power when the Holy Spirit comes on
you; and you will be my witnesses in Jerusalem, and in all
Judea and Samaria, and to the ends of the earth.*

—ACTS 1:8

OVER THE NEXT few months, the Power Group weekly early morning
Bible study meetings continued to grow, and Graham made every
effort to attend as many of these meetings as was possible with his
already busy work calendar. He was eager to spend time in God's Word,
but this hour of praying together with his staff was building a strong and
dedicated team.

It was in February of 2002, only four weeks prior to the second Day
of Repentance and Prayer, when Craig Meizenheimer had been the guest
speaker at one of the Bible study meetings. Due to prior commitments,
Graham was unable to attend that particular meeting. Craig had deliv-
ered such a strong message that many of those at the meeting wished that
Graham had been there to hear the words of the powerful young man.

People continued to encourage him to make time to hear this pastor
who spoke with confidence about God and the work of the Holy Spirit.
Two days later Craig was speaking at a venue close to the Power offices,
and Graham decided to set aside the time to go to this meeting. Knowing
that he was scheduled to take a telephonic interview with a national radio
station, he planned to slip out of the meeting for a few minutes and then
return as soon as possible.

On arriving at the venue in Stellenbosch, Graham approached the
young pastor and told him about his plan to slip out for about twenty
minutes to do the interview. Craig, warm and gracious in character, was
quick to respond and encouraged Graham to do his business and then to
return. He was going to pray for the fifteen men who had gathered and
was trusting God for a time of worship and intimacy. As a young believer,
Graham continued to hunger and thirst for more knowledge of the Lord;
he would read the Scriptures, spend time in private prayer and media-
tion, and learn from leaders in the Christian community. This morning

he knew that Craig was going to minister in prayer to the men who had gathered, and he was eager to listen and to learn. With little knowledge on the teaching of the Holy Spirit, Graham did not want to miss too much and so was thankful when he felt the vibration of his phone. He knew that the time for the interview had come, and once that was over he would be able to return to the meeting.

About twenty minutes later he walked back into the room, and as he entered he stopped at the door. What he saw was a sight that both mystified and intrigued him. He was expecting to see the men sitting or standing in prayer, waiting on the Lord, but as he entered he saw almost all the men lying flat on their backs. In that instant he was overwhelmed with an urge to turn and run, but he stayed, wanting to discover what had happened while he was out of the room.

As the men had stood in prayer they had received a touch from the Lord and were not able to stand in His holy presence. There was a quietness about the room as Graham entered. Gently closing the door behind him he walked down the side of the room, and just as he went to take his seat, Craig noticed him returning. He walked over to Graham and asked if it would be in order to pray for him. With downcast eyes and his hands clasped in prayer, Graham never even looked up at Craig, he simply nodded his head and asked the Father to reveal Himself and His love.

> Prayer does not fit us for the greater work, prayer is the greater work.[1]
> —Oswald Chambers

Craig raised his hand and placed it on Graham's shoulder, and as he did, Graham felt as though his legs could not hold the weight of his body. His legs buckled under him. Resisting at first, unsure of what was happening, he tried to remain standing, but within a split second he had fallen onto the soft carpet. As he lay there, he could hear his breathing increase, and his body shook with a tremor as though the current of an electric shock was moving through his body. What was this? He needed to stand and regain control. As he stood, he reached out to stabilize himself, and once again Craig put his hand on Graham's shoulder. Within an instant he was once again on the floor. Again the lack of control, again the electric shock, and once again he staggered to his feet as soon as he could muster the energy to pull himself off the floor. For a second time he stood and faced the young pastor, who without any fuss leaned forward and almost whispered in his ear, "Graham, God is not finished with you yet."

This time there was no possibility of taking control. For over one and a half hours, Graham lay on the floor and in those minutes experienced the presence of God like he had never done before. After a few moments of silence his breathing became more labored and strained. With every exhalation of breath it seemed as though the impurities of his body and life were being pushed out of him. His breathing became even more intense until it felt as though his entire body had been cleansed from the inside out, and all that remained was an outer shell of skin. Then, as he grew accustomed to the emptiness, he felt as though God took him by the feet and shook him again and again. Just like before, every movement seemed to be part of the cleansing process. It felt as though this took hours; he was being drained, squeezed, and purified. God was preparing His vessel for a message that would soon reverberate around the globe.

No sooner had the cleansing stopped than the rhythm of his breath once again began to change. No longer short and urgent, he inhaled long and steady breaths of clean fresh air. This air seemed to penetrate into every limb, organ, and cell. The old was gone and the Holy Spirit was filling with the new. The presence of the Lord felt tangible, and quietly Graham basked in this state of peace and newness, but all too soon the quietness of his soul was shattered with an excruciating pain. He lay on his back with arms stretched out, and as he lay, the base of his spine began to burn with a pain that was almost indescribable. As he gasped for breath, he imagined the pain a woman has to endure at childbirth and waited for the next surge of agony. As he lay writhing with pain, he heard a voice that seemed to reverberate from the core of his being. The voice was amplified, intense, and penetrating. The words were simple but clear. There was no mistaking their message.

Several times the voice said, "I am the spine, I am the spine, I am the spine." Next the booming voice said, "I am the head of the spine, I am the head of the spine, I am the head of the spine." Several times more the voice said, "I am the King, I am the King, I am the King." And finally without any pause the voice continued and declared, "I am the King of kings, I am the King of kings, I am the King of kings."

Feeling an intensity of emotion that he had never before experienced, Graham lay as if lifeless and with no desire to leave this holy place. As he waited, the moment soon extended into minutes, and he began to see the appearance of the shape of Africa being drawn around his outreached body. His feet touched the tip of Africa at Cape Town while his head rested in Egypt on the northern limits of the continent. As he lay on the ground, a physical sensation of pins and needles moved from below his feet up into his chest region and stopped under his armpits. His outstretched arms traversed the widest part of Africa reaching from west to east. After a few minutes of silence, he experienced the distinctive feeling of more pins and needles, this time moving from the tips of his fingers to the top of his head. He lay at the heart of his beloved continent and watched as his arms seemed to extend beyond the borders of Africa's land. Further and further they stretched until it seemed as though his arms reached out across the globe.

In an instant he knew that these arms represented the Father's arms and His love for a lost and hurting world. Then slowly and gently the arms stretched out across the breath of the world and then began to come together in an action that circled the globe. Lovingly as though giving a caress, God pulled the world closer and closer into his chest. And then as a young mother would carefully embrace a newborn baby, so the Father held His world close to His heart. The gentleness, compassion, and love were overwhelming. This was God the Father, nurturing His world. This was a visual picture of the Father's heart of God who, despite the lostness of His children, held them and wept for them. Tears of joy, unconditional love, and acceptance flowed from His eyes. The depth of emotion that Graham experienced was immeasurable, and the realization of God's unconditional love for His created world was forever imprinted on his heart and soul: "For God so loved the world that he gave his one and only Son, that whoever believes in him shall not perish but have eternal life" (John 3:16).

> There is not in the world a kind of life more sweet and delightful than that of a continual conversation with God.[2]
> —Brother Lawrence

God's love was overwhelming, and Graham did not want to leave that sacred place. For many minutes he lay and basked in the presence of his heavenly Father, and when the time seemed right, he stood slowly to his feet. As he steadied himself on a chair, he knew without a shadow of doubt that God had revealed Himself, and as the custodian of that revelation, he would need to walk in humility and obedience. It was in that moment of time that Graham came to understand that Africa, through a spiritual revival starting in the south, would become the light and hope of the nations.

As Graham thought and meditated on the images of this detailed vision, he believed that he was seeing with clarity the interpretation of the word of the Lord to him. The first stage of the vision had already taken place in the city of Cape Town in 2001.

Within weeks the second phase would become a reality as eight other South African cities joined in prayer, but it was as he lay on the ground that he received the most detailed instruction. Southern Africa was next to join in this move, and then the entire African continent was to be invited to participate in a time of repentance and prayer. Each stage of the movement correlated to the tingling sensation he experienced as it moved up through his physical body. And then finally, as his entire body had been engulfed with the presence of the Lord, so the entire world was to come together in unity and prayer at the foot of the cross. As he sought for clarity of thought, he was able to say with confidence that he believed, "Africa, once the continent of darkness, disease, sickness, and suffering, was soon to become a Light to the World."

This was not going to be political revolution or an economic renewal but rather a spiritual revival that would start at the tip of the continent and would progressively move up through Africa and then onwards and outwards around the world. And as this revival moved across the globe, God the Father would continue to pull the world close into His heart. He would love, cherish, and save His world and His people.

12
A NEW WIND BLOWS

If my people, who are called by my name, will humble themselves and
pray and seek my face and turn from their wicked ways, then will I
hear from heaven and will forgive their sin and will heal their land.
—2 CHRONICLES 7:14

I AM PRAYING FOR Africa. Are you?" was the slogan that hundreds of young runners wore on their t-shirts as they ran into the eight stadia around the country on the second Transformation Day of Prayer on the twenty-first of March 2002. They had already run hundreds of kilometers, but today was the day when the Walk of Hope ended in celebration and rejoicing. Running into the various stadiums, they lifted flags and banners and carried messages of hope from the people of South Africa. In every stadium the crowds erupted into cheers and shouts of encouragement, as they acknowledged the passion and determination of this next generation to play their part in the transformation of South Africa.

In 2001, forty-five thousand people had gathered to pray in one city, the city of Cape Town, but in 2002 in Johannesburg, Durban, Bisho, East London, Port Elizabeth, George, Mossel Bay, and Wellington, the vision expanded to touch the nation.

At exactly 2:00 p.m., Graham Power stood beneath a canopy stage at Newlands and welcomed the people praying together in Newlands. He extended a greeting to the hundreds of thousands who were linked via satellite to the other eight stadia. He acknowledged those watching in hospitals and prisons and from Europe and east Africa, including the Democratic Republic of Congo and Kenya. Today was the fulfillment of the next stage of God's vision. Christians from southern Africa were turning to God, and the invitation was being extended north to the rest of the continent. No sooner had Graham extended the words of invitation and made the bold proclamation that southern Africa would join in 2003, than he wondered what made him make that statement when he knew that it was not possible.

In the city of Port Elizabeth in Telkom Park, Bishop Mvume Dandala exhorted those gathered to remember that the law alone would never make us respect one another. He said, "It is Christ and Christ alone who touches me and makes me a better person. It is Christ alone who has the power to save us, and that is the reason why we are standing together today in South Africa asking God to make us a better people."[1]

Michael Cassidy continued the theme of discovering the power of Christ to save as he presented a clear message of salvation through Christ's death on the cross. At every stadium, men, women, and children responded to this message and asked God to forgive their sins. Transformation was starting in the hearts of the people as God began to prepare for renewal and revival.

During the weeks leading up to this second Day of Prayer, God kept directing Graham to 2 Chronicles 7:14: "If my people, who are called by my name, will humble themselves and pray and seek my face and turn from their wicked ways, then will I hear from heaven and will forgive their sin and will heal their land."

As he pondered and prayed about the significance of this verse in the prayer movement, Graham determined that the words of this verse would be embroidered onto every red armband handed out. This verse would become the guideline for prayer and repentance. The steps involved were clearly defined: first God's people needed to humble themselves in acts of repentance and forgiveness. Next there needed to be a willingness to turn from wicked ways and urgency in calling on the Lord. And then He would hear from heaven and heal the land. Healing the wounds of this fragmented nation would not be an easy task, but with God's directions the blueprint of the Transformation Africa team pointed the church in the direction of salvation, repentance, prayer, and healing.

> A servant of the Lord stands bodily before men, but mentally he is knocking at the gates of heaven with prayer.[2]
> –John Climacus

Around the nation, people prayed for needs specific to their community, but in every venue, the overriding theme was a spiritual request for personal and national transformation. As the Day of Repentance and Prayer came to a close, thousands were challenged not to let these few hours be an event in isolation but rather the beginning of a lifestyle that would change the spiritual climate and landscape of their country.

The first invitation to a Week of Generosity was in 2002. People were encouraged to share with those less fortunate than themselves. The idea for this initiative had come from the prompting of the Tshwane churches in the northern region of South Africa, where they had gathered together for a Week of Bounty. The caring and generous spirit of local churches at this time was used by God to restore broken relationships in many communities. Local churches had been designated as drop-off zones, and within days of the Day of Prayer, these churches, halls, and garages were filled to overflowing. People who had needs were able to come and take, while those who had were encouraged to keep giving. Mothers brought their children and allowed them to pick out clothes for school, and fathers were able to take home beds, cupboards, and even refrigerators for their family. The church began to follow the example of the church in Acts, and as they did, a spirit of joy captivated the hearts of believers.

Graham Power called the entire Transformation committee and organizers of the various events together for a time of thanksgiving at the Power Headquarters in Cape Town. As the team gathered around the tables, there was an excited buzz of conversation as everyone wanted to share his or her experience. As part of the evening program, individuals were given the opportunity to share with the group their personal testimonies of thanksgiving and praise.

One after another, men and women quickly strode to the microphone eager to give God the glory for what He had done on March 21, 2002. John Eachus, a member of the Transformation Africa committee, shared that his wife sat in a protected corner of the stadium, and while they were praying, her mother reached out and touched her shoulder. As they looked up, they felt a breeze blow across their faces and saw the soft material of their scarves move in the wind. Lifting their hands, they realized that there was not a breath of wind in the stadium, so tangible was the presence of the Holy Spirit. As John shared this story, others related similar experiences throughout the venue.

No sooner had the day been celebrated than planning for the following year began. The year 2002 had only been the second phase of the vision God had given Graham, and there was no doubt in his mind that the next phases of southern Africa and then the continent of Africa were crucial to the fulfillment of the vision—this would be the outstretching of the Father's arms around the globe, just as it had been in the vision.

Dawie Spangenberg had flown to Cape Town in order to attend the report-back meeting and returned home, satisfied that he had completed his commitment to assist in the planning of the 2002 Walk of Hope. The Walk had been a success, but he did not have peace that his involvement had been completed. He needed God to reveal His plan for their lives. By this stage, Dawie had finalized decisions regarding his business and was in the process of establishing another company with two other Christian businessmen.

Every week they would gather on Wednesday and Friday mornings for prayer and to ask God for wisdom, not only for the emerging company but also for their role in the Transformation Africa Prayer Day.

One day while they were praying together, Dawie looked up at the wall map of South Africa. To his surprise, he felt as though he were seeing a vision. He glanced away, wondering what was happening, and then looked back, realizing that they were indeed illuminated. Keeping his eyes fixed on the map, he leaned over the desk, grabbed a pen, and quickly wrote down the names of the towns and cities that seemed to be flickering with a bright light.

> Do not pray for easy lives. Pray to be stronger men. Do not pray for tasks equal to your powers, pray for powers equal to your task.[3]
> —Phillips Brooks

Casting his eye down the list, he counted forty names. In an instant he knew that these places were of great significance for the growth of the Transformation Day of Prayer. The three business partners turned to one another and with one voice agreed that their company was going to be a part of this mighty move and that they would willingly sacrifice both time and finance in order to ensure that they were a part of what God was doing. As they continued in prayer, they decided that Dawie would keep his position in the new company but the other two partners would release him for ministry. As they did that, they would also assist with the financial obligations and budgets that Dawie would incur over the next two years.

As soon as the meeting was over, the men shook hands, and this simple exchange of greeting was a seal on their commitment to each other and to the Transformation Africa prayer movement. No sooner had the men left the prayer meeting than Dawie wrote a three-page letter outlining a strategic plan that he felt the Lord had given him; this plan would enable them to reach not only at least forty towns in South Africa but also ten countries in Africa. He hesitated for just a moment before he faxed the letter to Graham Power, as he had not been asked to do it; but after just a moment's reflection, his confidence grew as he felt the inner assurance that this was exactly what God wanted him to do.

On receiving the communication under the heading, "This is how I think we can do it," Graham Power smiled and immediately recognized the intentional and positive attitude of his business friend. There was a confidence and an assurance about the fact that reaching South Africa and Africa was possible and there was already a plan brewing on how to make God's vision a reality. Graham requested that Dawie and Bennie Mostert from Jericho Walls meet in Pretoria, to discuss the way forward. The meeting was arranged for a few days later, and both men viewed each other with a certain amount of suspicion and caution. Bennie wondered what this businessman knew about reaching South Africa with a message of prayer, and Dawie wondered if Bennie knew how to motivate a strategic plan.

Dawie arrived at the meeting a few minutes early and waited for the appointment. He determined that he would just say what he believed God had shown him, and then he would leave and communicate directly with Graham Power. The conversation was short and cordial, as both men are not given to small talk. Quickly getting to the point, Dawie told of his vision and how he wanted to target forty cities in the country. He continued to explain how the city names had been illuminated on the map and how his partners were going to support his involvement in motivating the nation to pray.

Without a word, Bennie called his secretary, who produced a list of city names. Only a few weeks previously, they too had been asking God where they should focus their attention for the development of 24/7 prayer watches. As they prayed, they wrote down the names of forty cities and towns. In an instant a spirit of anticipation stirred within the hearts of both men, and it took them only a few seconds to scan down the list and recognize that this was the identical list of names. Jericho Walls had an additional three names, but every other city and town was repeated on both lists. As they exchanged gazes, they realized that this was God talking to both of them.

God had supernaturally revealed to two men, one from the business domain and one from the church, exactly the same list. The message was clear. This was to be a partnership, and God had given revelation to them both. The church needed the direction and purpose of business, and the businessmen needed the prayer vigils of the church. Not only were the two lists confirmation that this vision was growing as God was drawing together His team of co-workers, but that unity was going to be a powerful weapon in the extension of God's kingdom in South Africa and Africa.

It was evident that God had revealed the names of the next target points, but would the church in those cities be willing to participate? The only way to be sure was to invite the leaders to a gathering where they could share their vision, their needs, and where they could clearly receive the impartation of the vision for a day of prayer. Knowing that a letter would not have the same impact as a personal invitation, Dawie determined to travel to as many cities as possible. He wanted to see the leaders and invite them to this important meeting. As he traveled the great distances between the forty cities, Isebel transformed their family home into offices for Transformation Africa. She put two desks into their living room; one held a computer and the other a fax machine. Over the next two years these rooms and the Transformation office at Power Head-quarters would become the command center for the prayer day and the Global Day of Prayer.

It was with a sense of great expectation that Graham and Dawie waited to see who would finally attend the planning meeting on the twenty-ninth of May 2002. To their amazement, nearly eighty leaders once again gathered in the Power Group meeting room. This was evidence that there was a new wind blowing throughout the nation. As men and women met from different denominations and cultures, they began to discover the joy of true fellowship. This show of unity would become the catalyst for the third stage of the Transformation Africa Day of Prayer.

13

AFRICA FOR CHRIST

I will give them singleness of heart and action.
—JEREMIAH 32:39

FOR SO MANY years African leaders have listened to the ideas of others, submissively nodded their heads, and then continued to do things the way they have always been done. The Transformation Africa team acknowledged this fact and wanted to ensure that there was buy-in from a grassroots level. Churches and communities had to believe in this call to prayer. They needed to actively participate and own the process; otherwise, it would become yet another good idea within the kingdom of God. In order to facilitate a time for active listening and engagement, it became crucial to gather as many leaders as possible from the continent. African leaders needed to discover the joy of praying together, of moving in a spirit of repentance, and together discovering the way forward.

This concept of *ubuntu* or togetherness is such a natural leadership style for the people of Africa that it was decided to organize a prayer summit in order to facilitate this discussion and planning for the future. While God had given the vision to Graham Power, he realized that in order for this vision to move across the continent, the people of Africa needed to own the vision. As a businessman, Graham listened long and hard to the concerns of African leaders and did not want to make the same mistake of paternalistic leadership.

> God never gives us discernment in order that we may criticize, but that we may intercede.[1]
> —Oswald Chambers

Once again the invitation was extended. This time the net was broader, and Christian leaders from across the nation and surrounding African countries were invited. They were invited to not only hear about the instruction but also to participate in the development of a vision and a mission statement. Unity was becoming the repeated theme at every meeting, and it seemed as though God the Father was well pleased with every decision made. As the event grew closer, so did the feeling of anticipation. With

220 South African and 9 African leaders pledged to attend, this was to be a significant gathering in the history of the church in South Africa.

On the opening night of this gathering, Dr. Bruce Wilkinson, prompted by the Holy Spirit, led the gathering in a time of repentance and confession. There was silence in the room as Christian leaders opened their hearts to God and one by one went forward and knelt in humble confession. There was no need to cover old sins as men turned to one another and confessed sins of adultery and idolatry. This was a holy time, a solemn moment as the Spirit of God moved among the leaders, calling them to purity and fresh commitments to the lordship of Christ. It soon became evident that if God were going to bring revival and renewal to the people of South Africa, He would first need to start the process in the lives of the spiritual leaders of the nation. There was a somber reverence to this meeting, and on later reflection, many acknowledged that this was a turning point. This was the time when God started calling His church and the leaders to new levels of holiness.

Crucial to the stages of personal forgiveness were the times of individual and corporate repentance for the sins of apartheid committed by the white churches, leaders, and communities of South Africa. This issue, although dealt with before, was one that kept rising to the surface. Sometimes people would become impatient and want to know how many times it is necessary to express remorse for the sins of the nation. Each time Graham Power heard this discussion, his heart would break with the realization of the fact that while the laws of apartheid had changed, the scars were still very evident. Quietly he would give the wise answer, "Not seven times, not even seventy times seven times, but until the pain has subsided, and only then will there be no need to ask for forgiveness any more."

On several occasions during this conference, the main meeting would end, and men and women would refuse to leave the venue. Sitting on the uncomfortable chairs, they waited in silence. For hours they prayed, crying and trusting for revival to break out across the land.

As the body of Christ met together, prayed together, and walked a road of humility together, they were able to discover a vision and mission statement that clearly communicated God's heart for the people of Africa. By the end of the Bela-Bela conference, the vision, "Africa for Christ," and the mission statement, "Transforming Africa as we mobilize the whole church, community by community, nation by nation, with the whole gospel of Jesus Christ," were adopted by all the delegates.

Not content to merely talk about transformation, leaders were asked to make a personal pledge so that prayer and transformation could become a reality right across the continent and not just remain a good idea. Delegates signed a commitment to participate in annual days of prayer and fasting, to establish 24/7 prayer watches in their communities, to disciple and teach in and through the local church, and to begin saturation church planting. The call was great, the cost was high, but there was no doubt that in order for true transformation to take place, God's children needed to be willing to pay the price. They needed to be willing to feel the pain and to declare their desire to see transformation in every domain of society.

By the time the delegates departed after three days of prayer and repentance, they knew that the message they were taking back to their local churches was a message of hope and reconciliation.

Driving home, Graham pondered all that had taken place at the conference and made a silent pledge that he would be willing to pay the price and to be obedient to God—no matter the cost. Little did he realize that within a few months he would be able to act on this pledge and would have to bear the consequences of this important decision.

14

THE TIDE BEGINS TO TURN

*Do not use dishonest standards when measuring
length, weight or quantity. Use honest scales and
honest weights, I am the Lord your God.*
—LEVITICUS 20:35

A S THE SOUTH African economy battled against the winds of change and doubt, many successful businessmen and women became fearful for the future, and in a desperate bid to make provision for their families and secure their inheritances, they started illegally taking money from the country and investing it in off-shore bank accounts or in overseas properties. Graham and Lauren, like many others, had been part of this group of South Africans who had invested funds in offshore accounts.

Preparations continued in earnest for the 2003 Transformation Day of Repentance and Prayer. As the plans escalated, so did the budget projections and expenses. A decision was made to hold two fundraising banquets where the body of Christ would be given the opportunity to participate in giving toward the Day of Prayer. Johannesburg and Cape Town were the two cities that would host these events.

November 2002 was the date set for the Cape Town dinner. It was a black-tie event, and as guests stepped into the beautiful hall, there was a feeling of great excitement and expectancy. The vision had grown, the needs were great, but together the body of Christ could make a difference.

Dr. Bruce Wilkinson was the invited speaker, and it was his responsibility to lead the crowd in a time of giving. His message was an encouragement for Christians to humbly walk in submission and intentionally turn away from sin. At the end of his message, he invited Christians to come forward and make pledge offerings toward the expenses for the Day of Repentance and Prayer. The money raised would be used to provide logistical support in South Africa and Africa to carry the message of the Day of Repentance and Prayer to as many people as possible. The finances would be invested in the commissioning and duplication of the DVDs and videos produced by Media Village.

The time of giving continued for nearly thirty minutes. Every now and then, men and women would break into spontaneous songs of worship. There was no hype or fanfare, as people came forward and handed in their pledge cards. This evening raised nearly 3.1 million rand. This was the largest figure ever raised at a fundraising dinner. As Graham stood on the platform and received the pledges, he was so aware of the Holy Spirit prompting him to lead by example.

Returning to the table at the end of the giving time, Graham leaned over to Lauren and whispered to her that they needed to sort out their overseas investments, the most precious of which was their holiday house in Spain.

Knowing the determination of her husband, Lauren put her hand onto Graham's arm and asked him not to make any public announcements until they had discussed this issue with their children.

Graham and Lauren wanted to live a life of total obedience, and their home on the beautiful island of Mallorca was their place of refuge and family holidays, but even this had to be surrendered to God.

As Graham started asking his financial advisors for advice on how he could bring the money back to South Africa, and how he could declare the gain for taxation, they shook their heads in amazement and said that it was far easier getting it out of the country than getting the money back in again. The Power family had already discussed the implications of this decision, and they all stood behind their husband and father.

Then in February of 2003 during the annual South African Budget Speech, Mr. Trevor Manuel, Minister of Finance, extended a Grey Money Amnesty for all South African residents who had invested funds in offshore accounts in contravention of the tax laws and exchange control regulations of the government.

The Grey Money Amnesty provided transgressors an opportunity to "come clean" and declare their offshore investments. Any person who took advantage of the amnesty would avoid any future risk of incurring liability for previous contraventions of exchange controls or failure to declare income for tax purposes.

This announcement came as a complete surprise; there had been no advance warning, and yet this would be a window of opportunity for the Power family.

Graham smiled as he read the *Financial Times* because he had already made the decision to declare all his offshore finances, no matter what the cost.

Just like Abraham, who had been willing to sacrifice his son Isaac, Graham had been willing to offer his most prized possession in obedience, and then when it seemed as though they would have to lose this house, God made a way for them to be able to keep it. Since that time, each visit to Spain reminds the Power family that God needed to know the degree of their obedience, and every visit becomes a special time of celebration and thanksgiving.

While this decision had been made in the confines of their family and financial advisors, it would soon have serious ramifications for the Transformation Africa movement.

Three days after the budget speech and the announcement of the amnesty period, the Johannesburg fundraising banquet was held. As the Johannesburg meeting came to an end, the crowd rejoiced as the pledged figure exceeded one million rand. No sooner had the applause subsided than Graham stood behind the podium, took the microphone, and made a pledge of personal financial transparency.

In a soft voice with almost monotone precision, he told the crowd that over the years of apartheid and financial embargo he had done what many other South African businessmen had done. He had transferred money to offshore accounts and had made foreign investments. Some of these investments included their holiday house in Spain, a boat, and other luxury purchases. He told them of his discussions with his family and their joint decision to declare the earnings and to pay the price, no matter the cost.

He continued to tell the audience of Mr. Trevor Manuel's decision to introduce an extended amnesty period, and that he and Lauren were going to take full advantage of this offer. He invited others to do likewise, so that as a nation we could all discover the joy of transparency and accountability and living a life that is beyond rebuke.

It only took a few minutes to make these statements, but the impact would last a lot longer.

Early on Monday morning Graham received a phone call from his mother, who had read the local newspaper reporting on that fact that he had as a Christian businessman raped the country of millions.

Driving to work, Graham could see the headline displayed on many lamp poles. This headline drew the nation's attention to his public confession. Gently, Graham reassured his mother, giving her the details of the overseas financing. He told her that he felt this decision to "come clean" had been part of his personal promise to God. Finally he consoled and reassured her, but he knew that there would be many skeptics who would not be silenced quite as easily.

Putting down the phone, he slowly sat on the chair and stared at the receiver. In an instant he knew that this was part of the cost. Quietly he prayed, *"Lord, let me walk this road with integrity and never compromise my witness for You. I have acted in obedience. I am prepared for the consequences, but I want to know that before You and man I have a clean heart and clean hands."*

This event was the most embarrassing moment of Graham's life, yet in a miraculous way it would prove to be the catalyst for an unashamedly ethical instruction that God would reveal in years to come.

15

SHARING THE BLESSING

They will be called the Holy People, the Redeemed of the Lord.
—ISAIAH 62:12

ONTHS OF PRAYER and preparation finally bore fruit on the first of May 2003 when seventy-seven South African cities joined the thousands of believers praying together in Newlands Stadium in Cape Town. As Christians gathered to seek the Lord's face, twenty-eight African nations joined this mighty move.

This day of prayer had been preceded by a weeklong chain of 24/7 prayer meetings across South Africa, and as the sun set on the eve of the third day of prayer, hundreds of young people gathered for prayer in an event called "Fast Forward." Young people expressed their desire to see God move in their lives. As they gathered for prayer, they prepared a spiritual highway across the continent of Africa. Believers

> When God is ready to do a new thing amongst His people, He sets them praying.[1]
> –James Edwin Orr

from every denomination met and prayed against the Goliaths that face the continent of Africa. HIV/AIDS, poverty, economics, and gender issues were all top of the agenda in most of the meetings.

In the city of Cape Town, the African Children's Choir opened the meeting at Newlands Stadium with a song of hope, boldly declaring that with God there is a better tomorrow. Graham Power encouraged the crowd with a prayer of dedication. Confidently he prayed aloud, "Father see our hearts and hear our prayers."

As a declaration of unity, people in the stadium stood to their feet and declared their intention to become a praying people. In reality they were all writing history as they witnessed the fulfillment of the third stage of the vision.

Within hours after the conclusion of the Day of Prayer, reports of God's presence started coming in from all over the sub-Saharan region.

The nation of Uganda has a history of civil war and alarming statistics of HIV/AIDS prevalence rates, but May 1, 2003, was a day when the church decided that they would make a spiritual stand against the powers of darkness that have kept the people in bondage. As the sun blazed down, thousands of Christians slowly made their way into the sports stadium right in the heart of the capitol city of Kampala. Women wearing outfits made from bright material and matching headdresses carried young children on their backs and joined the body of Christ in repentance, prayer, and worship. The minutes soon became hours as Christians wept and wailed, pleading with God for the needs of their nation. Many reports said that there was an atmosphere of a spiritual awakening right across the land.

In another city north of the capital, downpours of rain threatened to dampen the spirit of unity and faith. Yet despite the heavy rainfall, hundreds of people danced in the streets and followed a vehicle through the center of town. Slowly moving through the crowded streets, believers played worship music and encouraged others to join together and to trust God for the redemption of their nation. Together they declared peace in Africa. This was a day of unity among many denominations, most of whom had not worshiped together for years. A local pastor declared, "The hearts of men and women have begun to be softened toward the gospel. The glory of God is now vivid, and we thank God for the person to whom God gave the vision to pioneer this prayer network across Africa."

This person was of course Graham Power, and while he was completely unaware of the people who were praying in Uganda, God was not. God their heavenly Father knows them all by name, and He hears their prayers. Graham's acts of obedience were bearing fruit right across the continent.

Driving home from Newlands Stadium at the conclusion of the Day of Prayer, both Graham and Lauren experienced the quiet serenity of knowing that they were right in the center of God's will, and nothing, not even the success of business nor the fame of public recognition, could have replaced the personal joy they both experienced. Arriving home they sat down to a simple supper of soup and crackers and then turned on the television to watch the recording of the day's events. Despite the exhilaration and exhaustion of the day, they spent the next three hours watching a replay of the Transformation Africa Day of Prayer. With every link across the continent and with every prayer prayed, Graham knew that this was indeed fulfillment of the vision and instruction he had received from God. Feeling totally overwhelmed by the significance of the Day of Prayer, Graham spent time in God's Word, and it was well past midnight before he finally closed the Scripture and went to bed.

Yet another Week of Bounty was held around the nation. This week continued to be the opportunity to tangibly express obedience to the Lord's words when He said, "By this all men will know that you are my disciples, if you love one another" (John 13:35.) Local churches around the country became points of distribution as people started sharing with the less fortunate.

Church halls were filled to overflowing with clothes, furniture, refrigerators, and even cars. People from impoverished communities were able to go to churches around the country and take goods according to their needs.

In one community hall, a young mother stood openly weeping as she filled her bag with white shirts, grey shorts, and long black socks. She had never been able to afford to buy her children school uniforms. As she looked at the mountain of donated clothing, she remembered the prayer she had prayed standing among the thousands of people in Newlands stadium. She had specifically asked God to hear her cries. She needed clothing so that her children could attend school looking like the others. She was weary of the shame that she carried because her children did not have school uniforms. Every day she kept choosing to feed her family rather than buying the required clothing. God heard the cry of her heart, and on the following Monday morning her children proudly went to school wearing their new school uniforms.

16

AFRICA'S CANOPY OF PRAYER

How beautiful on the mountains are the feet of those who bring
good news, who proclaim peace, who bring good tidings, who
proclaim salvation, who say to Zion, "Your God reigns!"
—ISAIAH 52:7

MANI IS A uniquely African movement focusing on catalyzing African National Initiatives and the mobilizing of the resources of the body of Christ toward the fulfillment of the Great Commission. MANI is not an organization but is rather a network of organizations, people, and vision. Within the African context the concept of networking is an important strategy for unity. It is in discussion and partnership that people are given dignity and feel respected. There are few people who understand this concept as well as the soft-spoken New Zealand missionary, Ross Campbell. Ross lived and worked in West Africa for more than twenty years. Over this time he not only grasped the issues pertinent to leadership in Africa but also won the trust and confidence of leaders across the continent. His love for the people of Africa was never diminished by his knowledge of the needs and problems facing the continent.

As Ross sat in the 2002 meetings at Bela Bela, he committed to sharing his contacts and knowledge with the Transformation Africa team. His high level of credibility in Africa opened doors for Transformation Africa to attend many conferences and meetings over the next two years. On each occasion they were able to present the vision of Africa for Christ and invite every country in Africa to join in the 2004 Day of Prayer. As African leaders received this invitation, they immediately identified with the call and indicated their desire to be a part of this mighty move of God. This was Africa responding and believing that the vision of Africa for Christ could become a reality and not merely a mission statement.

It soon became evident that Ross Campbell was once again God's provision of the right person at the right time, and he became invaluable in motivating the continent to join together in prayer. As Ross traveled throughout Africa, he began to realize that the first of May clashed with many national rallies for Worker's Day celebrations. This meant that

stadiums were already booked and Christians were going to have a difficult time finding venues large enough to hold the expectant crowds of
people coming together for prayer. After discussion with church leaders
across Africa, a unanimous decision was made. The fourth day of prayer
would be held one day later on Sunday, May 2, 2004.

With MANI as a key partner, Transformation Africa was guaranteed
a grassroots participation across the continent. Little by little, with every
e-mail sent and received, their hope increased that the entire continent
would indeed participate. The Transformation office worked tirelessly,
trying to make contact with the few outstanding countries, and by the end
of February only five countries were yet to register their participation.

Dawie and Isebel Spangenberg were very aware of the potential criti-
cism that Transformation Africa could receive when quoting numbers of
people attending or countries participating. This prompted them to be
extremely diligent in record keeping. No event, region, or country was
registered until the office had confirmation of a venue booking and the
contact details of the person responsible for the event. This decision was
certainly one inspired by God because for every cynical request of veri-
fication, the team was able to produce details that have satisfied even the
most skeptical observer.

Praying over the map of Africa, it became obvious that the outstanding
countries were those up in North Africa, many of which are known
as "closed countries." While these nations may be closed to the public
presentation of the gospel, God by his Holy Spirit is still at work, and
believers in these nations were just waiting, believing in faith that one
day there would be an opportunity to join with the body of Christ in
unity and prayer.

In an attempt to see the fourth stage of God's vision fulfilled, the entire
continent needed to be joined together—that meant all fifty-six countries.
With the outstanding four or five countries, the team knew that despite
being very close to their goal, they had not yet reached the intended
mark. Determined to actively assist in getting those nations to participate, Bennie Mostert and a group of Egyptian intercessors arranged to
send a small delegation of prayer warriors to each of these nations.

Cautiously these men and women entered into unknown territory, and
then to their utter surprise and amazement, they found believers gathering in every "closed" nation. News of the Day of Prayer had infiltrated
the body of Christ, and even though they had not officially registered,

these believers were determined not to be left out of this historic day. They had planned to meet in family homes or secret places, but there were no doubts that they would join Africa in prayer.

Within hours of discovering these small cell groups of praying men and women, the news was received at the Transformation Africa offices, and immediately shouts of jubilation and thanksgiving filled the air as the team danced around hugging each other. Some even shed tears of joy. God had answered their prayers; Africa would indeed pray as one. Together they thanked the Lord as they finally registered all fifty-six countries in Africa.

> Let the fires go out in the boiler room of the church and the place will still look smart and clean, but it will be cold. The Prayer Room is the boiler room for its spiritual life.[1]
> –Leonard Ravenhill

With only a few days to go before May 2, initiatives and movements continued to grow, and young people dedicated themselves to twenty-four hours of prayer, seven days a week. Many high schools around the nation of South Africa hosted Boiler Rooms of prayer, and reports kept coming in of the prophetic words that God was giving the emerging generation of young intercessors and prayer warriors.

Entering a Boiler Room is an exciting experience, and it certainly has no semblance to any traditional prayer meeting. The walls are covered with papers that contain graffiti or world maps, newspaper headlines or words of praise and worship. Colored strings and ribbons hang from the ceiling, and it is here that young people peg their petitions and requests as a creative reminder of their time spent with the Lord. In a distant corner there is a quiet place where it is possible to sit and silently worship God.

While the exact details of a Boiler Room may vary depending on the location, the one element that always stays constant is the desire of this generation to bring the needs of a hurting world to God their Father. They are passionate and serious in their commitment. It was many of these Boiler Room prayer meetings that prepared the way for the day when all of Africa would finally pray together.

As the Transformation Africa prayer movement began to grow, Graham and the team made a very important decision that would ulti-mately contribute to the high degree of ownership that many countries experienced as they planned and organized their own day of prayer. Every town, city, or nation was invited to express intercession and worship in a way that was culturally relevant. There were no prescribed programs. There were no requests for dignitaries or political figures to be held in high esteem. It did not matter whether people where gathering to pray in stadiums, school halls, old age facilities, or family homes; this was a day of personal prayer, repentance, and thanksgiving. The only request from the Transformation Africa committee was that all venues pray a united prayer for Africa. This Prayer for Africa is based on the words of Matthew 6:9–13:

> Our Father in heaven, hallowed be your name,
> Your kingdom come, your will be done on earth as it is in heaven.
> Give us today our daily bread.
> Forgive us our debts, as we also have forgiven our debtors.
> And lead us not into temptation, but deliver us from the evil one.

All across Africa the preparations had been made, and finally it was the day—May 2, 2004. This was the realization of the fourth stage of the vision.

History was written as every country in Africa joined in prayer and worship. Denominational boundaries were removed, hurts forgiven, and reconciliation experienced as the body of Christ turned in unity and lifted their voices to the King of kings and Lord of lords. Worship songs gathered like sweet incense as the tongues and tribes of Africa celebrated their salvation and then presented the needs and petitions to the throne of grace.

Across the nation of South Africa, 273 towns and cities gathered in prayer, while at Newlands Stadium in Cape Town, Graham Power walked to the podium and with a heart filled with thanksgiving once again welcomed the crowd. His voice gently shaking with the joy of realizing the faithfulness of God, Graham warmly extended a welcome to all who were present at the stadium or watching on live broadcasts around the world.

"Friends, today we are at stage four of the five-stage plan that God revealed for Africa. And now at this moment, a whole continent is joining together in prayer with you and me." These words ignited a thank offering of praise and worship that started the celebration on this significant day.

Everywhere you turned there was a reminder of the Christian

commitment to repentance and prayer. The stadium was filled with hundreds of young people wearing the same white t-shirt that the youth had worn as they ran across the nation in the Walk of Hope. The printed words "I am praying for Africa. Are you?" prompted believers to keep praying for Africa.

The keynote speaker at Newlands was Ed Silvoso, evangelist and founder of Harvest Evangelism International. Standing tall behind the podium and flanked by two enormous blue backdrops that carried the Transformation Africa logo, Ed engaged the crowd with an interactive message of hope. His powerful voice lilted with a strong Argentinean accent as he proclaimed, "Today you and I, along with millions more, have been convened by God almighty to raise a canopy of prayer all over Africa. From Cape Town in the South to Cairo in the north, from Senegal in the west to Somali in the east, and to the Democratic Republic of Congo in the center, today, here, now, Africa is being covered in prayer."

As Ed proclaimed these words, the Newlands stadium erupted into a time of thank offering to God, and as they did, it seemed as though the echo ricocheted around the continent.

The image of Africa being covered in a canopy of prayer caught the imagination of millions, and every individual felt that they were holding their corner of this mighty covering. And as they did, a spiritual highway was forged from Cape to Cairo. Over the years there have been so many prophetic words about the linking of these two significant places on the African continent, and the Transformation Day of Prayer was making all those visions a reality.

As the event unfolded in Cape Town, millions of people joined the praise and worship as they watched their television screens, listened on radios, or downloaded images on their computers. A live interactive broadcast was produced from the SABC recording studios in Johannesburg. Small production teams from Media Village went to various locations across Africa. At a prearranged time, telephonic links were made to numerous cities, giving up-to-date reports. Each account was filled with a sense of growing realization that Africa was indeed covered in prayer.

As Graham left the stadium and drove along the freeway back to his home in Somerset West, he listened to Ed Silvoso and Bruce Wilkinson reflect on the day. It was only when Ed reached over and touched his shoulder saying, "My brother, do you realize what just happened today? Today for the first time in history an entire continent has joined in prayer." As he listened to these words, there was a clear moment of revelation when he realized what God had done through his life and through simple acts of obedience.

To the north, Egypt is a land with much tradition and history, and yet it still faces denominational mistrust and separation. On May 2, however, all seventeen denominations came together to pray for their land. Reports were received of over 120 gatherings of Christians in locations across the country as well as in the Western Desert, Morocco, and Mauritania. Many of these intercessors had prayed through the night in preparation for the Day of Prayer.

In the east African country of Uganda, camera crews recorded children leading their parents in hours of prayer for those suffering with HIV/AIDS. They wailed and repented for the bloodstains on their land and asked God to heal the nation of Uganda and restore her people as a God-fearing nation.

In the West African country of Ivory Coast, a significant event was recorded when four pastors stood in front of hundreds of people and asked forgiveness for division and disunity. Together they said, "The church in Ivory Coast has not exercised her power and authority. Today we are here to repent. We are sorry, Lord. Forgive the leaders. Forgive the church. Forgive us for being divided. We thank you for reuniting us and that this union can be reinforced through transformation."

Hundreds of people in Ghana sat in the blazing sun under makeshift canvas shelters, where they had gathered for five days of prayer and fasting. As worship filled the air, men and women pulled small white handkerchiefs from their pockets and waived them in the air as they danced on the red dusty earth. Nothing, not even the high temperatures, could dampen their spirits.

Then at three o'clock South African time it happened. Programs halted, the music faded, and together Africa prayed the responsive prayer for the continent. It is estimated that more than twenty-two million Christians stood in unity and prayed these words for the land and people of Africa. This was a holy moment; it was a solemn moment as the body of Christ spoke with one voice. The prayer may only have taken about ten minutes to read, but spiritually the gates of heaven had been besieged, and believers stood confident that God would hear the cries of Africa.

It is written in Isaiah 66:8: "Who has ever heard of such a thing? Who has ever seen such things? Can a country be born in a day or a nation be brought forth in a moment?" Thousands declared their belief and made statements of faith that this day was a day of new beginnings for Africa.

As in previous years, accounts of answered prayer, miracles, and transformation soon began to flood into the Transformation Africa offices.

Like many countries in Africa, South Africa has had to deal with the ongoing violence between tribes and people groups. The small town of Piet Reitef in the province of Mpumalanga, South Africa, eagerly told their story of unity and forgiveness as the local taxi association sponsored all the transportation to the stadium. Hundreds of people were collected en route and taken to a stadium that knew neither color nor denomination.

While this event had focused the attention of the world on South Africa and also the continent of Africa, it was obvious that there was no way to control the incredible pace with which the vision of a Day of Repentance and Prayer was beginning to move across the globe. The spark had been lit, and now the flame was beginning to burn all over the world. Within a very short space of time this event had moved from being a well-organized day of prayer to becoming a movement that would soon traverse the globe, and where every nation and tongue would have the opportunity to stand before the throne of grace in repentance and prayer.

Linda Ma, a successful businesswoman from Hong Kong, had stood together with South Africans in prayer in 2004, and as she raised her hands in worship, she declared that she would return to Hong Kong and would hire a stadium for the 2005 event. This act of faith was a foreshadowing of what was yet to come, when one year later thousands and thousands of believers turned toward China and prayed for that nation.

17

AFRICA'S INVITATION
TO THE WORLD

And I, because of their actions and their imagina-
tions, am about to come and gather all nations and
tongues, and they will come and see my glory.

—ISAIAH 66:18

No sooner had the Transformation Africa team completed their records for the 2004 Day of Prayer than they realized that there were so many requests from around the globe for information on how to get involved as a praying nation. The vision had spread like wildfire. What had started as a small spark at the tip of Africa had spread across the continent; now the world wanted to participate, and Africa was eager to extend the invitation.

As Africa invited the world to join in the next Day of Prayer, Graham and the team realized that this event could no longer be called the Transformation Africa Day of Prayer. It was time to extend the vision. At that moment in time, the Global Day of Prayer was birthed. The vision was so large and the growth so unprecedented, that people around the world started to own the vision as God's plan for their city or nation. Never before in recorded history had the whole body of Christ joined together for a day of global prayer.

The Global Day of Prayer had one goal: to see every nation join together on one day of united prayer, to pray for the salvation of the lost, to do acts of repentance, and to turn the hearts of the people back to God.

The events of 9/11 in New York City shook the world. In an instant, fear seemed to grip the hearts of millions. The known became the unknown, and ideas of safety and security all seemed to melt away under the threat of oppression and the tyranny of fear. Around the world, Christian leaders realized that there was an urgent need to unite ministries, prayer networks, and organizations. In the midst of uncertainty, the church had a profound opportunity to speak the truth of God and bring hope where a spirit of hopelessness was prevalent.

The International Prayer Council (IPC) came into existence just after the 9/11 attacks and determined to be part of bringing unity and change. They desired for the body of Christ around the world to unite and speak with one voice. This decision would give the church both authority and credibility, where disunity had weakened the power of a unified church.

Transformation Africa started working closely with IPC from the start of the second Transformation Africa Day of Prayer, when almost three hundred prayer network leaders from each of the fifteen world regions gathered in Cape Town. At this meeting they resolved to pray together for the glory of God and work toward the healing and transformation of the nations.

The next strategic gathering of the IPC was held in Thailand. Both Dawie Spangenberg and Graham attended this meeting. Flying together, they determined that this was a God-given opportunity to extend an invitation from Africa to the world. This was Africa's moment, and the invitation was simply a request to join in a Global Day of Prayer. Despite Graham and Dawie's enthusiasm, they were surprised at the skeptical questions that came from the group. Men and women showed concern about the logistical planning of such an event. Leaning back in his chair, Graham remembered that the same issues had previously been raised nearly five years ago when he first presented the vision to the local pastors of Cape Town. Was this history repeating itself? No sooner had he thought those thoughts than the peace of God took control of his mind, and he quietly acknowledged that this was God's dream, and His will would be done with or without the IPC.

> You never have to advertise a fire.[1]
> —Leonard Ravenhill

God was in control, and He had indeed paved the way for the global invitation. In the early hours of the following morning, John Robb, chairman of IPC, was woken by the Spirit. God spoke to him about the true significance of the Global Day of Prayer, and the vital importance of supporting it. John wasted no time in putting together a PowerPoint presentation that not only traced the history of the Transformation Africa Day of Prayer but also presented ideas for future expansion and growth for the Global Day of Prayer.

Early the next morning, leaders listened to his confident words. He closed his presentation by saying, "There is no way that the IPC can ignore this move of God. It is way too big to disregard. If the IPC does nothing else but take the GDOP vision and run with it, we will have achieved more than if we achieve all the mid-term goals that we have set for ourselves to do."

There was silence in the room. The significance of these words began to resound in every heart. This truly was a move of God, and they were invited to be part of it. The river of prayer, repentance, and intercession was moving at an incredible pace, and if they neglected this opportunity it would pass them by.

The silence was broken by a series of hearty amens, and then without any further discussion or hesitation there was unanimous agreement. Once again God had been faithful. The words of encouragement the Spirit had given Graham had come to pass. This was God's vision, and He was leading the way. The invitation was now official. Africa invited the world to pray, and in a significant moment through IPC, the world accepted the invitation.

This event proved to be a watershed moment. At the close of the meetings in Thailand, the entire gathering stood and anointed a small team of men to be the bearers of this invitation to the world. Bennie Mostert, John Robb, and Bob Bakke were to join Graham and Dawie traveling to as many nations as possible and personally inviting them to be part of the Global Day of Prayer.

As the meeting closed, John Robb gave Graham a small plastic holder of mustard seeds. This small bottle contained thousands and thousands of tiny black seeds, each one the size of a pinhead. Looking down at the bottle of seeds in his hand, Graham was reminded of the Lord's promise that if we have the faith of a mustard seed, we can move mountains. In the most incredible way, God had already moved mountains. Africa had already joined in prayer, and now the world would become part of this significant event.

Ever since that meeting, Graham has carried the bottle of seeds in his briefcase, and wherever the opportunity presented itself, he would open the bottle and plant seeds in the earth or give a few to believers, asking them to join this venture of faith. Christians were encouraged to trust God for an increased faith in the power of prayer.

This small team immediately moved into action and began to visit as many countries as possible. After a few weeks of planning, it soon became evident that there was simply not enough time to ensure that every country got a personal invitation. They needed another strategy.

Each member of the group prayed and trusted God to show them how to maximize the impact of the Global Day of Prayer and how many people as possible could receive the invitation and the details for convening the event.

Bob Bakke then reminded Graham of the National Religious Broadcasters Conference (NRB) that was to be held in the USA.

"This would be an ideal opportunity to present the vision of the Global Day of Prayer," Bob explained, "as every major radio and television broadcasting station from around the world will be there."

Once again God provided the ideal vehicle for communicating the vision to as many people as possible. Travel plans were soon set in motion, and the team arrived in Anaheim, California, filled with a great sense of expectation. Their suitcases were filled with a compilation DVD that contained all the report-backs of previous years as well as all the documentation required to host a prayer day. Once there, however, they realized that it was not that easy to get a presentation spot in any of the plenary sessions as the programs had been planned months in advance. For just a moment, their spirits sank as they tried to understand this obstacle. The team got together and stood in the foyer of the conference center and prayed, "God we know that this is Your vision and Your instruction. We commit this meeting to You and ask that You make a way for the DVD to be shown at this conference. We need You to make a way where there seems to be no way. Amen."

Within a few hours, Graham had been introduced to the event organizers, and after telling them about the vision and extending the invitation from Africa, they agreed to let the GDOP team show the thirteen-minute report-back that had been produced by Media Village. This was a direct answer to prayer. Not only were they able to show the DVD, but also they did not have to cover the high cost of having a presentation shown in a plenary session. As the house lights faded and the opening music came onto the large center screen, each of the GDOP team silently said a prayer of thanksgiving.

The response was immediate. The world of Christian media got the picture. Understanding the power of media, they pledged to be part of communicating this message. Hundreds of stations, broadcasters, and affiliates agreed to share the message and broadcast as much information as possible about this event. Within one session, the breadth of international communication had exponentially increased. Suddenly the impossible seemed not only possible but also probable. Within days, the Transformation Africa/Global Day of Prayer Web sites began to get countless hits as event coordinators signed up from around the world.

> In the last days, God says, I will pour out my Spirit on all people. Your sons and daughters will prophesy, young men will see visions.
> —Acts 2:17

As people around the world began to realize the spiritual significance of the world praying together, it became imperative that more and more prayer be part of the planning and preparation. As coordinators communicated about the Day of Prayer, they started calling for ten days of night-and-day prayer preceding the event; then for one day of global prayer; and finally for ninety days of blessing. This time of preparation, prayer, and blessing soon became known as 10:1:90.

The city of Jakarta, Indonesia, launched the ten days of prayer prior to the first Global Day of Prayer in 2005. On this occasion, 120,000 Christian believers gathered in one stadium. Thousands who were not able to enter stood outside the stadium and listened to the live broadcast signal, while seventy-six other stadium gatherings in the country connected via satellite feed.

> The least of you will become a thousand, the smallest a mighty nation. I am the Lord; in its time I will do this swiftly.
> —Isaiah 60:22

It is significant to remember that only months prior to this meeting, Indonesia had captured the hearts and minds of the world when the devastating tsunami swept across the land killing thousands of men, women, and children. An enormous flame was lit, and hundreds of young people took a torch and marched around the stadium. This symbolic act represented their hearts' cry to carry the light of Jesus into the darkest places. The entire stadium stood in unity, and despite their pain and loss, they worshiped and asked for salvation to come to their nation. The evening closed with thousands of worshipers raising their voices to the music of "How Great Thou Art."

On every continent, young people began to catch the vision, and reports were received from more than 360 venues that joined in prayer meetings called "A Whole Night for the Whole World." Entering into these venues, it was evident that the Spirit of God was moving in the hearts of young people who had boldness and a willingness to do daring feats for God. Praying through the night, fasting, and worship were all expressions of their willingness to stand in the gap for their generation. They were eager to take the adrenaline-seeking passion of their youthful years and focus it on seeking the will of God for their lives.

As the sun rose over Fiji on the fifteenth of May 2005, the first Global Day of Prayer, President Ratu Josefauluivuda welcomed the world. "Lord, we have disobeyed your Word. We are sorry." His simple words of repentance set the tone for what was to be the largest prayer event in all recorded history.

As the sun moved through the various time zones around the world, 156 countries participated, and one-by-one they took their place in this historic Global Day of Prayer. Perhaps for the first time in history, the world was on the brink of fulfilling Isaiah 45:6: "From the rising of the sun to the place of its setting men may know there is none besides me. I am the LORD, and there is no other."

Over recent years, the Presidential Square of Taipei, Taiwan, has been the venue for numerous meetings and political rallies, but on this day it was the meeting place for nearly thirty thousand believers. Just as the Global Day of Prayer commenced, the heavens opened and Christians stood for hours in the pouring rain. Thousands of white and yellow rain jackets protected their skin from the downpour, while their spirits joined the river of praise that was sweeping around the globe. The storm was not able to disrupt the spirit of unity, prayer, and worship that filled the square. Waiving brightly colored flags and long palm fronds, the body of Christ prayed for the salvation of the lost and the needs of their nation. Cultural dancers and songs filled the air, and with every song sung and prayer prayed, these Christians knew that they were writing history.

In Hong Kong a significant breakthrough occurred when Christian leaders were able to secure the Hong Kong Stadium for thirty thousand believers for a daytime meeting. Later that evening, another ten thousand joined together in a second stadium for a time of prayer and worship. These two events were of great significance and encouraged the church to believe that God was beginning to do new things in difficult places. Disunity had also been prevalent in the churches of Hong Kong, but after this day of prayer, leaders declared, "It was moving to see pastoral staff come together in unity to declare that they belong not to a certain church or denomination, but that they belong to and serve the church of Hong Kong."[2] This historic prayer meeting closed as the people of Hong Kong stood to their feet, raised their hands, and prayed a blessing on the people of China.

While thousands were gathering in stadiums, city squares, cathedrals, or churches, many others were meeting in secret places. Reports were received from believers who met in Qatar, Vietnam, Yemen, Bahrain, Cambodia, Jordan, Tunisia, and Somalia. These are countries where professing your faith may well cost you your life. The fact that persecution and punishment are very real threats for civil disobedience in countries closed to the gospel, Christians still decided to meet together and join the world in prayer.

In one country where it was too difficult to find a place to meet, Christians organized several vehicles and drove around their city for hours praying and interceding for their nation.

When the sun finally set over the Hawaiian Islands, more than one hundred million Christians had met and participated in the first ever Global Day of Prayer. There was no doubt that the main objective of the Global Day of Prayer had been achieved. Their desire to pray with one voice, asking God to bless and heal the nations of the Earth and to collaborate as one body as an instrument through which God can answer prayers had been achieved.

18

FOR GOD SO LOVED THE WORLD

*He will turn the hearts of the fathers to their chil-
dren, and the hearts of the children to their fathers.*

—MALACHI 4:6

S THE GLOBAL Day of Prayer team continued to meet under the leadership of Graham, many committee members expressed their concern to strengthen the youth involvement in this move of God. While the youth had already participated in GDOP, it was decided that an intentional focus needed to be given to encourage the youth to express their love for Christ. The body of Christ needs their youthful exuberance and also the revelation that God is giving to this younger generation. It was decided to appoint a global youth coordinator. Etienne Piek, who had already been actively involved in various prayer movements and was the secretariat for the International Prayer Council (IPC), was unanimously elected to take this important position. Etienne has a love and passion for youth. He sprang into action right way and started looking for new and creative ways to motivate and include young people.

Immediately he began to challenge the youth to not only discover their place in the GDOP but also to actively participate in various aspects of leadership and presentation. On June 3, 2006, the day preceding the second Global Day of Prayer, youth around the world led a "Global Day of Compassion." Their purpose was not only to talk and pray about transformation, but also to be actively involved in the process. Young people were encouraged to go into their communities and neighborhoods looking for the difficult places and then to ask how they could serve. This act of servanthood was used by God to break walls of hostility and bridge the gap between young and old.

In Ireland, hundreds of young people took to the streets and worked in gardens, painted walls, planned holiday clubs, and shared the love of Christ through their deeds. The results were amazing. Doors that had been closed for so long opened, and years of misunderstanding began to fade away as young and old started seeing the power of love in action.

As the youth began to take their ordained positions at various locations,

God used them to speak peace and blessing to the older generation. In numerous venues it was the children who led the prayers of repentance and asked their parents for forgiveness. These prayers were used by God to turn the hearts of the children back to their fathers, and the fathers back to their children.

> **Everyone was filled with awe, and many wonders and miraculous signs were done by the apostles. All the believers were together and had everything in common.**
> **–Acts 2:43-44**

The second Global Day of Prayer was held on June 4, 2006. The body of Christ rejoiced when 199 of the 220 countries in the world participated in this event. It is estimated that more than two hundred million Christians participated in this time of repentance and prayer around the globe.

Back in Cape Town, Graham and the GDOP team marveled at the faithfulness of God. With every new confirmation of participation, their spirits soared and their faith increased as they anxiously waited for the time when every nation on the Earth would join together. While that target had not been fulfilled in 2006, it was certainly an item of prayer for 2007.

Over the next few weeks, Isebel Spangenberg and the Transformation office were inundated with reports and testimonies of what God had done around the world on June 4, 2006. Stories included accounts of salvations and repentance, reconciliation and forgiveness, healings and miracles. Just about every country had their unique account of how the Spirit of God had revealed Himself to the body of Christ.

As the Transformation team sat and reflected on the work of God around the world, they were reminded of the vision that God had given Graham. Together they contemplated the image of the young mother gently embracing a child and holding her close. The faith stories from around the world were all reminders of the fact that God loves His world, and He longs to heal the pain and to draw men and women to Himself so that all may discover true transformation.

19

MAY YOUR KINGDOM COME ON EARTH AS IT IS IN HEAVEN

Command those who are rich in this present world not to be arrogant nor to put their hope in wealth, which is so uncertain, but to put their hope in God, who richly provides us with everything for our enjoyment. Command them to do good, to be rich in good deeds, and to be generous and willing to share. In this way they will lay up treasure for themselves as a firm foundation for the coming age, so that they may take hold of the life that is truly life.
—1 TIMOTHY 6:17–19

A S THE DAYS moved into months, Graham found himself spending more and more time in God's presence. Through his continued study of God's Word, he found himself asking questions about the role of Christians in the transformation of society. No longer content simply to motivate prayer initiatives, he started asking God to change his thinking so that he would be in complete alignment with God's heart for the lost and for nation transformation.

The more he read the Scriptures, the more convinced he became that salvation is the doorway to a personal relationship with God, but once Christians become children of God, they are called to share their faith and then to be nation-changers. Christian men and women are expected to be people who can assist in fulfilling the Lord's Prayer: "[May] your kingdom come....on earth as it is in heaven" (Luke 11:2, NKJV).

There were some days when it seemed that the answers were so difficult to find, and yet he believed with all his heart that God had written a blueprint for the church to follow. October 6, 2006, was one of those occasions.

The International Transformation Network (ITN) was holding a two-day conference in the city of Cape Town. Ed Silvoso had flown directly to South Africa after a week in Indonesia. While he was in that nation, known for its corruption, illegal business, and government dealings, Ed had led wealthy business and city developers to commit their city to God.

These influential businessmen signed a pledge to not pay or receive bribes and to live lives free of corruption.

Ed recalled the details of this landmark signing, and while he talked, the men and women who sat in the air-conditioned room listened in awe. God was beginning to stir up something in their hearts. If a nation infamous for its corruption could even begin to make an effort towards ethical practices, then surely it was something that could be repeated around the world.

> You may say to yourself, "My power and the strength of my hands have produced this wealth for me." But remember the Lord your God, for it is he who gives you the ability to produce wealth, and so confirms his covenant, which he swore to your forefathers, as it is today.
> —Deuteronomy 8:17-18

The Rupert family is one of the wealthiest families on the continent of Africa, and Hanneli Rupert-Koegelenberg had been called by God to play a role in the process of reconciliation. At the end of the first day of meetings, she whispered a few words to Graham, expressing a desire to actively demonstrate what God had laid on her heart. As a white, privileged, Dutch Reformed church member, she believed that God wanted her to humble herself and wash the feet of men who represented those who had been exploited by the wealthy during the apartheid years, dating back to 1652 and to the earliest settlers in southern Africa.

The next morning during the session, with little fanfare and with no attention being drawn to herself, Hanneli invited Rev. Hendrik Saayman to join her so that they could express true servanthood through this simple action. She took a bowl of warm water and asked Pastor AyJay Jaantjies to sit on the stage so that she could wash his feet. Next she called another pastor from the largest informal settlement in the city to sit beside him.

AyJay lowered his head and felt the pain of his people who today are known as the Khoi-San or First People of the Land. Hanneli felt the warm water run through her fingers; she looked up into the face of AyJay and saw tears running down his cheeks. As they stood and embraced, it was as though a stronghold was broken in the heavenlies. Black and white, rich and poor, stood together at the foot of the cross, and God was honored. This simple act of obedience became the catalyst that God used to put the attention back on Himself and His purposes for South Africa and Africa.

Repentance was the theme of the afternoon as people walked across the room, found other believers who were different than themselves, and took out small packets of wet-wipes to wash each other's hands. Every now and then someone would start crying, and an embrace would follow, as words of forgiveness were spoken. God was healing hearts and preparing the way for renewal and restoration.

The conference concluded with a gala dinner where the Cape Town mayor, Mrs. Helen Zille, was the guest of honor. Graham had prepared two large pledge cards, which clearly stated the conference delegates' pledge to no longer practice corruption or to be part of the paying and receiving of bribes. There were 180 signatures from marketplace ministers and 40 from pulpit ministers. No one present could have imagined that this would be the beginning of the birthing process—the start of a new move of God in our times. Africa was being challenged to break the shackles of poverty, and the starting point would be the elimination of systemic corruption. It was clear that systemic poverty could never be dealt with until systemic corruption was eradicated.

It had been a long day at the conference by the time Graham finally got home, but despite his weariness, he kept imagining the potential impact of Christian businessmen and women in the marketplace.

After several hours of restless sleep he woke at about 4:00 a.m. He felt a surging sensation of electricity passing through his body. Immediately he recognized this as the same sensation he had experienced when God had imparted the second vision of a mother embracing her child.

Lauren woke as she felt Graham tremble in the bed beside her. She thought her husband was having a heart attack, and as she leaned over to look at him and put her hand on his chest, she heard his voice say in the darkness, "It is all right. I will talk to you later."

The first instruction from God was to invite the whole world for a time of prayer. This time had been the season of equipping and laying down a solid prayer foundation around the world. This was, however, to be a new time, a time for a new vision and yet another challenge.

Lying back against the pillow, Graham prayed, asking God to show him the next step in the process for nation transformation. For almost three and a half hours Graham lay on the bed, and as he lay, he felt the ongoing sensation of electricity pulsating through every fiber of his body. He knew that God had heard the cries of his heart, and so he waited. As he waited, his mind was filled with a great sense of excitement and expectation.

Several hours later, once the sensations left his body, Graham sat up in bed and began to write the thoughts and impartation that he had received from God. The first wave of transformation had been a wave of prayer. This wave that started as a small current in his home city of Cape Town had become a mighty wave that quickly swept across the globe. The church had heard this call. No sooner had they heard than they obeyed. Believers started to pray in multitudes from every nation and tribe as never before in the history of the church. Now was the time for another move of transformation.

The next step in this active demonstration of Christ's power for trans-formation was a new wave of ethics, values, and clean living. This second wave, just like the prayer movement, was going to have its source in Africa and would soon move across the continent and then the entire globe. This would be the beginning of a new season and the prophetic fulfillment of "turning from our wicked ways."

Then there was the third wave, which was not revealed in as much detail but would follow the first two waves. The third wave would no longer merely be a wave but rather a tsunami of revival, positive living, transformation, and an awesomely positive experience of living a life based on God's principles. It was in that moment of time that Graham clearly understood the significance of all three waves.

Looking up from his Bible and notebook, Graham could see that Lauren had fallen back to sleep, so he decided not to wake her. He needed to cement the words in his mind and soul. This was a challenge that was so large that, as with the first vision, only God would be able to turn the tide of corruption across the nation, Africa, and then the world.

As the early morning light started to filter through the curtains and the room began to fill with sunshine, Graham woke Lauren and told her the details of this new revelation. Lauren paid close attention to every word that Graham was saying. She knew that God had already done an extraordinary miracle in the life of her husband, and she certainly was not going to throw any seeds of doubt on these words. As she listened, deep in her heart she knew that this was yet another clear instruction from the Lord.

As they sat and spoke about the details of this new vision, they both knew that their personal lives and the Power Group of Companies would have to be above reproach. They would have to live lives completely free of compromise. If Graham was going to raise the flag and promote a life that spoke of ethics, values, and clean living, he would have to present a personal example of every one of these qualities. As they talked and prayed about this new instruction, they knew that this would become the season of complete ethical living.

A meeting was rapidly called that morning, and Graham shared with the intercessor leaders, his close family, Ed Silvoso, and the other leaders present about this new revelation.

A few months later, Graham received and read a report from Transparency International, a Berlin-based nongovernmental organization that said its global corruption barometer during the year of 2006 showed bribery was most prevalent in Africa, where an average of 36 percent of those surveyed said they or a member of their families had paid a bribe in the past twelve months. Latin America was next, with 17 percent of those polled saying they had bribed someone recently. In Russia and the former Soviet republics, the figure was 12 percent. This report was the confirmation that Graham needed.

If Africa was to reflect the character of Christ and wanted to eliminate systemic poverty, these issues of corruption and bribery would need to be addressed. Within a few days Graham called together his intercessors and submitted this vision to them. There was unanimous agreement that God was calling his church, the entire body of Christ, to purity and ethical living as an outward expression of internal transformation.

The more he meditated on the words of 2 Chronicles 7:14, Graham became convinced that the prayer movement that had covered the Earth through the Global Day of Prayer was part of the first wave of revival. This was an act of God's people humbling themselves, calling on His name, and seeking His face. Now it was time for the second wave of believers to turn from their wicked ways. The word *turn* seemed to shout to him of intentionality and purpose. God was saying that if His people would not only pray but also turn from their wicked ways, He would hear from heaven, forgive their sin, and heal the land. Both the seriousness and the impact of this revelation began to burn in his heart, and this self-made man, who had totally surrendered his life to the lordship of Christ, now began to lead the charge on breaking one of the most powerful strongholds of our time. The cost would be high and the challenge enormous. Just as before, he determined that each decision would be made in prayer and acted on with unwavering obedience and dedication.

In the days and months that followed, the Power Group of Companies was put under the ethical microscope, and wherever there was a hint of unethical dealings or questionable business procedures, they were highlighted and removed. A meeting was convened with 420 staff members who had all become shareholders in the Power Group, and together they committed to a focus on ethics. As a public demonstration of his intent to manage his company in line with biblical principles, Graham instructed his graphic artists to change the company logo. The words "Unashamedly Ethical" became an integral part of the design, and every business card, company sign, and construction board boldly made this statement of intent.

This concept of ethical behavior was well received in the Christian community, but Graham determined that this challenge was not just for Christians, it was also for the entire nation. After looking for the most suitable occasion to publically declare his intentions, he decided that the Power Group cocktail party would be the ideal place to launch this God-given idea. This annual event is attended by the city mayor, local and national government leaders, builders, architects, contractors, and clients serviced by the Power Group.

It is a well-known fact that the building and construction industry is no stranger to the issues of bribery and collusion. It was also known that before Graham had changed his company's conduct and started running his company on biblical principles that some individuals within the Power Group had participated in decision-making that was not in line with this new Unashamedly Ethical drive.

It was just after 6:00 p.m., with the venue filled to capacity, that Graham stood on the platform and projected the guidelines for running a business that was Unashamedly Ethical onto two enormous side screens. This was the first major public presentation, but he knew that this was what God was asking of him, and any hint of doubt or reservation disappeared the moment he started telling the more than one thousand people in attendance about the way forward. Once again large pledge forms were available, and 240 people signed their name to the Unashamedly Ethical document. The choice was clear: ashamedly unethical or unashamedly ethical.

Word soon began to spread around the city, and the challenge was extended, inviting other companies to sign the Unashamedly Ethical Pledge, which clearly stated their intention to avoid corruption and to begin a new wave of good values and God-honoring business practices. Graham used every opportunity to promote this document, and soon a database of companies began to grow, all of which were willing to submit to a high standard of ethical management and value-based transparency.

In accordance with the instruction, Graham followed each step, eager to see God's vision quickly become a reality. The challenge was being extended, and so the next step was to engage the services of an ombudsman to develop an Unashamedly Ethical electronic yellow pages.

The ombudsman ensures that all who signed the document are held accountable for their behavior and business dealings. Any reports received of unethical behavior are investigated and acted upon.

Today within the Power Group there is a clear course of action for anyone wanting to anonymously report on any form of corruption or unethical behavior. Once the investigation is complete, the report is made public, declaring the continued movement towards the elimination of corruption. Along with the reporting of unethical behavior, there are training sessions given to assist people to understand this new course of action.

The electronic yellow pages is becoming a fast-growing database that gives professionals and individuals the opportunity to exchange goods and labor, and do business with others who have sighed the Unashamedly Ethical Pledge.

After much prayer and consultation with leaders and intercessors, the following guidelines were established as a Charter of Conduct for anyone signing the Unashamedly Ethical document.

As an individual, businessperson, professional, or employee committed to transformation, I pledge:

To be ethical, operating in the highest integrity to produce and deliver superior products and services, including:

- Refusal to accept or pay bribes
- Paying taxes

- Paying reasonable salaries/wages
- To intentionally *invest in the betterment of my workforce and their families*
- To actively pursue the transformation of my sphere of influence and expertise in the marketplace
- To invest generously and sacrificially in the broader community with the focus on eradicating systematic poverty
- To purposefully connect with other companies, professions, and individuals to impact the world

As this second wave begins to sweep across the world, Graham believes the scripture "…then I will hear from heaven, and will forgive their sin and heal their land" (2 Chron. 7:14) is being set in motion, and we will soon experience the joy of seeing revival and the reality of living in a transformed nation.

20
HIGH PLACES

You who bring good news to Zion, go up on a high mountain.
—Isaiah 40:9

PLANS FOR THE 2007 GDOP were well underway when Graham and Dawie received a very unusual challenge from Etienne and a group of young Christians. While reading the book of Isaiah, some young people read the words, "You who bring good news to Zion, go up on a high mountain. You who bring good tidings lift up your voice with a shout, lift it up, do not be afraid."

Believing that this was a word from the Lord, they set their minds on finding the high places of the world. Daring to dream the impossible and not being afraid to ask why not, the youth issued a challenge to the older generation: "Let's take the words of Isaiah to heart. Let us join together old and young and go to the high places of our cities and nations and pray for God to bring transformation."

The challenge had been issued, and with very little or no hesitation, it was decided that a team of believers would challenge the highest point in Africa. Their goal would be to summit Kilimanjaro on the morning of the third Global Day of Prayer.

Immediately, plans and training began in earnest. While believing God for the faith to reach the summit, many hours of physical and spiritual training were required in order to be adequately prepared for this daunting task.

No sooner had the challenge been extended than the invitation went out for others to join the team and pray from the highest place in Africa. Forty people responded to the invitation.

Kilimanjaro stands tall at 5,895 meters or 19,340 feet, and Uhuru peak marks the highest point on the African continent. This mountain is also the tallest freestanding peak in the world. An international team with members from South Africa, America, Uganda, and Tanzania joined the group that had set their sights on praying from the highest place in Africa.

Standing at the Machame gate, many of the team shared their personal desire to see the transformation of Africa. Graham stood beside a Tanzanian porter and emotionally expressed his dream to see the dark continent of Africa become illuminated with the reality of the kingdom of God and to experience the love of Christ through the forgiveness of sins.

As the group picked up their backpacks and leaned on their walking sticks, a pastor from Uganda prayed for the climbers and porters, his passionate words encouraging them to see themselves as pioneers—men and women who would walk across the plains of Kilimanjaro praying for the needs and people of Africa. The next five days would be days of pain and perseverance, determination and dedication. After a time of short discussions about how the team would carry a wooden cross to the summit, and hearing the guidelines for communication and safety on the mountain, the team set out to conquer the summit.

Early every morning, Tom, the Tanzanian cook, walked through the camp and lightly tapped on the tent flaps. Putting a small bowl of lukewarm water outside each door, he encouraged the team to rise and come to the breakfast tent. Hours before the walkers awoke, the porters prepared a cooked meal consisting of porridge, eggs, toast, and warm tea and coffee. As the weary and sleepy men and women crouched their way out of their tents, they gathered at the foot of the wooden cross and prayed for Africa.

Every morning the team of climbers spent time in silence on their own or prayed together as a group. They asked God to protect them, but more than that they prayed that God would use them as individuals to bring about the change so urgently needed in Africa.

After five days of climbing, it was time for the final preparations. It was the night to summit the highest peak on the continent. After only two hours of sleep, Tom woke the group of climbers at exactly 10:00 p.m. and offered each person a cup of hot coffee or chocolate and a few dry biscuits. Standing in a circle with their small headlamps shining into the darkness, the team trusted God for their safety and for the people around the world who had already started praying together on the Global Day of Prayer.

The months of preparation and the days of climbing were finally going to bear fruit. At 11:00 p.m., the long, thin line of climbers began their ascent, and the words of Swahili songs echoed from the mountain crags. As they prepared for the final ascent, Lance, the leader of the group, said,

"These are the only guidelines for the night. Do not ask how long. Do not ask how far. Just walk until the sun rises and then you will be ready to face the last climb to the summit."

It was a long night; the effects of lack of oxygen and low temperatures soon began to take their toll. As the hours dragged, three were finally forced to turn back to base camp. Altitude sickness, exhaustion, and the extreme temperature had made it impossible for them to continue

As the sun rose on the eastern horizon, the darkness lifted, and rays of light began to set the clouds ablaze. Still the climbers slowly moved forward, step-by-step.

Stella Point was the final hurdle to be conquered. The summit was finally visible, but still they needed to reach the place where they would stand and join the river of prayer that was flowing around the world. One by one the team reached Uhuru Peak. A lonely signpost marks the spot. The final destination had finally been reached. Some of the climbers sank in exhaustion; lying on the snow, they completed the physical mission, but now was the time to spiritually stand in unity and prayer for Africa and the world.

A porter leaned against the wooden cross that stood high against the brilliant blue sky. The team joined hands as Graham led a time of prayer for Africa. Together they interceded for the lost and for the salvation of the people of this continent. With one voice they pleaded with God for reformation and transformation.

"Today," Graham prayed, his voice a whisper in the cold air, "from the rising of the sun over Fiji to its setting over the Hawaiian Islands, the world is gathering for this incredible Day of Prayer. We are not alone; we are part of this move of God. Together we are joining hundreds of millions of Christians around the world." Various team members held the flags of their nations and prayed for God to reveal Himself and for Christians to take their rightful place in the transformation of nations. After twenty minutes of prayer, the team began to disperse. Some of them felt an urgency to descend to a place where breathing was easier. Others lingered at the summit, savoring the moment and personally confirming their pledge to keep praying for Africa and to be part of the discipling of this mighty continent.

Kilimanjaro was not the only high place that was conquered on the 2007 Global Day of Prayer. There were many places around the globe where Christians joined the challenge to pray from the high places of their nations. In the nation of Zimbabwe, groups of men and women climbed the Matopos Mountains. The enormous boulders that lie scattered throughout this National Park were once the living places for the local Ndebele kings. In places the large smooth rocks are difficult to climb, but the team reached out and pulled their prayer partners over the rocks so that together they could summit the high place of their city. Many young people stayed long after the sun set; they lit a fire and prayed through the night, pleading with God for the urgent needs of their country.

In the nation of Brazil, groups of people decided they would also climb to the high places of their nation. Ascending the tallest buildings of the cities, they raised their hands and joined millions of believers around the world who were celebrating in their own culture and language.

Within hours of the sun setting on the western horizon, reports started flooding into the Transformation Africa offices. Individuals, nations, and tribes were eager to give an account of God at work in their country. This day had been a day of historic proportions. Giving accounts of God's faithfulness and recording the miracles were simply acts of worship and thanksgiving. These stories would soon be used to encourage others to participate in the 2008 Global Day of Prayer.

Media Village once again compiled a documentary entitled *God's Call to the Nations*. This twelve-minute documentary was translated into more than twenty-five languages, and an estimated five hundred thousand official copies were made. There is just no way of knowing how many people around the world watched the story and felt inspired to be part of history and join this global prayer movement in 2008.

21

SIGNIFICANT PLACES—GOD'S NEXT STEP...AND YOURS

At that time I will gather you; at that time I will bring you home. I will give you honor and praise among all the peoples of the earth when I restore your fortunes before your very eyes.
—ZEPHANIAH 3:20

IN 2007 CHRISTIANS prayed from the high places of their cities and nations, and in 2008 the challenge was to pray from the significant places of our world. In some nations this meant going into the economic centers of their cities, or into the halls of government. By this stage in the unfolding story of the global prayer movement, there were many partners and alliances with other ministries and movements.

Since 2002, when the second Day of Prayer and Repentance took place in Cape Town, God TV has partnered with GDOP and used their network to broadcast the prayer day around the world. In 2008 the partnership was further cemented when the entire day was anchored from their broadcast studio in Jerusalem.

God TV changed their broadcasting studio into an Upper Room, where they made an altar from thousands of prayer requests that had come in from around the world.

Graham joined Wendy and Rory Alec in this Upper Room, and together they hosted the live broadcast for nearly sixteen hours. This broadcast started at 6:00 a.m. Jerusalem time and continued until 9:00 p.m. that evening. Live feeds were received from numerous countries around the world, and millions of viewers were able to watch the entire day of prayer as it unfolded from sunrise to sunset.

In the studio a large world map covered one of the interior walls, and as each country sent in information, Wendy, Rory, or Graham would move to the map and pray for that nation. Internet messages, satellite connections, and phone calls made this an interactive live event. Numerous nations appointed a spokesperson for their region, and they were ready to give an account of the preparation that had preceded this incredible day. Stories of miraculous provisions for venues and finances kept flowing into the studio, and accounts of answered prayers created an atmosphere of rejoicing and thanksgiving. Around the globe, men and women began to see the power of God at work through His Holy Spirit.

As the sun set on the western horizon on May 11, 2008, there would be no way of ever knowing how many Christians gathered around the throne of grace and prayed together. What is known, however, is that this was the largest prayer meeting in all recorded history, and every believer who prayed added their prayer to the river of prayer and played a part in this historic day. It is estimated that more than three hundred million people joined together from 214 nations to spend a Day in Repentance and Prayer.

As these nations gathered, the words of Isaiah 66:18 seemed to echo from every corner of the globe: "And I, because of their actions and imaginations, am about to come and gather all nations and all tongues, and they will come and see my glory."

Not all 220 countries of the world joined in prayer in 2008, but the good news is that there is great anticipation that this incredible vision will soon be fulfilled.

The Global Day of Prayer's story has been one of vision and inspiration, and its rapid growth is a tribute to the fact that while it all started with one man's obedience, it has become a move of God. This movement does not carry the name of one man, it has no headquarters, and it is not bound by any hierarchy or country. It is the body of Christ anxiously waiting for God to save the lost and transform a hurting world.

Much like a young mother who conceives in joy, and then waits for the time of gestation to pass so that a new life can begin—so too the Global Day of Prayer has gone through a period of growth; but now is the time for the vision to become a reality. Now is the time for the body of Christ to rise up and lead the way forward in revival and transformation. There is no need to force the process, because the Spirit of God is moving in such a miraculous way that together we are all bearing witness to God at work in our cities and nations. There is no doubt that God is using His children around the world for such a time as this.

Together we have made history. Now that the first instruction of the vision is close to being fulfilled, the stage is set and ready for the second wave of values, clean living, and ethics to be ushered in so that we can finally see God "heal our land."

This is the time for the body of Christ and for the church to lead the way in fulfilling the Lord's Prayer when He prayed, "[May my] kingdom come....on earth as it is in heaven" (Luke 11:2, NKJV).

Looking back over the history of the Global Day of Prayer, it is clear that God has set out a blueprint for revival and nation transformation that is anchored in his Word.

> If my people, who are called by my name, will humble themselves and pray and seek my face and turn from their wicked ways, then will I hear from heaven and will forgive their sin and will heal their land.
>
> —2 CHRONICLES 7:14

It was during wave one that God called His church and children to humility, repentance, and prayer. This wave has been experienced as the entire world has gathered together on one day, the Global Day of Prayer. Wave two, which focuses on the instruction to turn from our wicked ways, is being realized as Christians begin to stand for righteousness and live lives that are unashamedly ethical. The third wave is yet to be experienced, but there is no doubt in the minds of millions of Christians that the entire world will begin to experience the abundant joy of lives totally surrendered to God. This is the abundance and satisfaction that Jesus spoke of when He came to give us life.

As this mighty move of God continues to grow around the world, and every nation, tribe, people, and language gather in prayer, repentance, and worship, there will soon be a multitude too great to measure. And as the body of Christ covers the nations of the world in prayer, a cry will be heard from north to south and east to west:

> Salvation belongs to our God, who sits on the throne, and to the Lamb.
>
> —REVELATION 7:20

The work has only begun! As the church begins to look toward a global celebration when the whole world will gather to give thanks, pray, repent, and seek God's guidance, together we are trusting that the Lord will continue to seek and save the lost, and transform the nations of the world.

This gracious miracle has caused the spotlight to refocus on Africa and her people. From Niger to Nigeria, Cameroon to the Central African

Republic, Rwanda to Kenya, and right through the heart of the Congo, God has stirred the hearts of men and women.

As the momentum of the second wave continues to increase, many people around the world are discovering that swimming upstream against the tide of corruption is not an easy feat. Graham believes that God has clearly shown that every time another person takes a stand for godly ethics and values, the strength of the current is diminished. The more we persevere, the greater the possibility of ultimately stopping the flow of collusion, bribery, and corruption. In most parts of the world there are prevailing circumstances that force people to swim in the dirty waters of corruption, but no one is forced to drink of that water.

Today is a unique moment in history. The global church has gathered for prayer; now it is up to every Christian believer to play his or her part in the transformation of families, communities, and cities.

God, our heavenly Father, longs to hold His children, to embrace His church, to nurture and protect His bride. He gave us the conditional promise that He would heal our land if we would turn from our wicked ways; now is the season to turn so that we may experience the rewards of this promise.

God's kingdom is extended on Earth every time a believer stands for righteousness and walks with integrity. This is your day. This is your opportunity to become a community transformer and nation-changer. Imagine the impact of an equipped and mobilized global church.

Surrender your life to the love of Christ, confess and repent for your sinful ways, and turn to your heavenly Father. Determine to be God's channel of blessing to a hurting world as you develop a daily lifestyle of prayer.

Be bold, be courageous, and play your part in the unfolding of the second vision. No one can stand for Christ in your family, business, school, or community except for you. God wants you for a time such as this.

God has miraculously used Graham Power to awaken a mighty army of prayer warriors from around the globe. If this is what God can do through one person, imagine what He can do if you and I join together with believers from around the globe. Together we can stand in the gap, stem the tide of corruption, and wait with eager anticipation for God to hear our prayers and heal our land.

This is an account of the incredible story behind the Global Day of Prayer. Looking back over the short history of this prayer movement, there is no doubt that the entire body of Christ can say with confidence that this supernatural display of unified repentance and prayer is of such significance that "it is not by might, nor by power, but by the Spirit of the Lord" (Zech. 4:6).

TO CONTACT THE AUTHOR

THERE ARE SO many stories—too numerous to tell in one account—of God at work around the world through the prayer ministry of the Global Day of Prayer.

If you have an account of answered prayer or a record of the history of the planning, coordination, and the Day of Prayer in your nation, please visit http://www.globaldayofprayer.com. We want to archive this incredible move of God with as many eyewitness reports as possible, so take a moment to share your story with millions of believers around the world.

If you are looking for resources for ethical living, or have a story to tell that bears testimony to either the effect or the results of living a life that adheres to the guidelines of the Unashamedly Ethical code of conduct and business ethics, please share them with us at: http://www.unashamedlyethical.com.

PRAYER FOR AFRICA (2004)

{ MAIN FOCUS OF prayer: To let the revelation of the Father's love, as demonstrated by His Son, Jesus Christ, transform Africa.) Based on John 17:1–26:

Father in heaven, today across the nations of Africa, we bow before Your throne of grace.

Thank You that through the death of Your Son, Jesus Christ, on the cross,

And through His resurrection,

You removed the hindrance of sin and made a way for us to be reconciled with You.

Today we acknowledge and declare that You are the one and only true God.

We accept the authority You have given Your Son, Jesus Christ, over all the people of Africa.

Congregation: *Eternal Father and Son, as we bow before You, we submit to Your authority over all.*

Lord Jesus, thank You for Your obedience to the Father's will.

Through Your life and conduct, Your sufferings and death, You revealed the Father's immense love for us.

We respond to that love with all our heart and soul.

In the light of knowing the Father's love, help us to love our neighbours as we love ourselves.

Congregation: *Eternal Father and Son, we love You with all our heart, mind, soul, and strength.*

Almighty Father, throughout Africa the evil one has sought to divide, steal, and destroy.

Let the knowledge of who You are and of Your love for us release a wave of true worship, forgiveness, and reconciliation in this continent. Break the power of the evil one.

Protect our faith and grant that we might be faithful witnesses of hope.

Congregation: *Father, as we draw near to You, we resist the enemy and all his strategies for this continent. Let Your Presence drive away the darkness.*

Father of all nations, as You sent Jesus into the world, so You have sent us.

Raise up the church in Africa to be a true representation of Your love and compassion.

Give us wisdom and courage to help the unemployed, the poor, the sick, the dying, the orphans, and the destitute.

May we never be ashamed to declare Your love for all those around us.

Congregation: *Lord Jesus, transform our hearts so that Your love and compassion may flow through us to those in need.*

Christ Jesus, today across Africa, we declare:

You and God our Father are the perfect demonstration of unity and love;

Our faith and trust in You as Savior made us one with You through the cross.

As we abide in You and You abide in us,

Let the glorious character of the Father's love be revealed through our lives.

May our love and unity be an expression of Your love for the people of Africa.

May we experience the full measure of Your joy as we daily live for You.

Congregation: *Lord Jesus, draw us into the unity You have with the Father and help us to be of one spirit, one mind, and one heart.*

Compassionate Father, thank You that we have a home with You in heaven.

As we represent You, the one and only true God,

May the world know and understand that You did not send Your Son to condemn them,

But that You love them even as You love Your Son Jesus.

May Your Name be glorified in the Church and the revelation of Your Fatherhood spread through this continent.

Congregation: *Loving Father, as we seek to obey You, reveal Yourself to our hearts. Today with Christians all over the world, and with the Spirit, we cry out:*

Come, Lord Jesus, Come!

Establish Your kingdom amongst us.

PRAYER FOR THE WORLD (2008)

They raised their voices to God with one accord.
—ACTS 4:24, AMP

Almighty God—Father, Son, and Holy Spirit,

Together with believers all over the world,

We gather today to glorify Your Name.

You are the Creator of heaven and earth.

There is no one like You, holy and righteous in all Your ways.

We submit to Your authority as the King of the universe.

We pray with one voice to enthrone You in our hearts

And to honor You before the world.

Congregation: *Lord God, You alone are worthy of our praise and adoration.*

Our Father in heaven,

Thank You for loving the world so greatly.

You gave Your only Son, Jesus Christ,

To die on the cross for our sins

So that we could be reconciled to You.

We are grateful to call You Father and to be called Your children.

Nothing can separate us from Your love.

Congregation: *Thank You Father, for adopting us into Your family because of Jesus Christ our Savior.*

Lord Jesus Christ,

You alone are worthy to open the scrolls of history,

For You were slain and have redeemed us to the Father by Your blood.

We confess that You are Head of the church

And Lord of all heaven and earth.

May people from every tribe and language become Your followers

So that Your blessing brings transformation among all peoples.

Let Your kingdom be established in every nation of the world

So that governments will rule with righteousness and justice.

And may Your Name be great, from the rising of the sun to its setting.

Congregation: *Jesus Christ, You are the Savior of the world and the Lord of all. Father of mercy and grace,*

We acknowledge that we have sinned

And that our world is gripped by the power of sin.

Our hearts are grieved by injustice, hatred, and violence.

We are shamed by oppression, racism, and bloodshed in our land.

We mourn all loss of life in murder, war, and terrorism.

Our homes are broken and our churches are divided by rebellion and pride.

Our lives are polluted by selfishness, greed, idolatry, and sexual sin.

We have grieved Your heart and brought shame to Your Name.

Have mercy on us as we repent with all our hearts.

Congregation: *God of mercy, forgive our sins. Pour out Your grace and heal our land. Spirit of the living God,*

Apart from You, we can do nothing.

Transform Your church into the image of Jesus Christ.

Release Your power to bring healing to the sick,

Freedom to the oppressed, and comfort to those who mourn.

Pour Your love into our hearts and fill us with compassion

To answer the call of the homeless and the hungry

And to enfold orphans, widows, and the elderly in Your care.

Give us wisdom and insight for the complex problems we face today.

Help us to use the resources of the earth for the well-being of all.

Congregation: *Holy Spirit, we need Your comfort and guidance. Transform our hearts.*

Lord Jesus Christ,

Because You were dead, but are now risen,

And the Father has given You a Name above all names,

You will defeat all powers of evil.

Tear down strongholds and ideologies that resist the knowledge of God.

Remove the veil of darkness that covers the peoples.

Restrain the evil that promotes violence and death.

Bring deliverance from demonic oppression.

Break the hold of slavery, tyranny, and disease.

Fill us with courage to preach Your Word fearlessly,

And to intercede for the lost faithfully.

Congregation: *Almighty God, deliver us from evil. King of Glory,*

Come and finish Your work in our cities, our peoples, and our nations.

We lift our voices in unison with believers from Africa and Asia,

From the Middle East and Europe, from North and South America,

And from Australia and the Pacific Islands—together we cry:

Congregation: *Lift up your heads, O you gates! Be lifted up, ancient doors, so that the King of glory may come in!*

As Your deeds increase throughout the earth,

And as Your blessings abound to all the nations,

They will seek You, asking, "Who is this King of glory?"

Together we will answer:

Congregation: *He is the Lord Almighty! Blessed is He who comes in the name of the Lord!*

Come fill the earth with Your glory as the waters cover the sea.

The Spirit and the Bride say:

Congregation: *Amen! Come, Lord Jesus!*

NOTES

FOREWORD
1. Juan Oritz, *Living With Jesus Today* (Lake Mary, FL: Strang Communications, 1982).

CHAPTER 2
1. Andrew Murray, *With Christ in the School of Prayer* (New Kensington, VT: Whitaker House, 1981).

2. Mary Garnett, *Take Your Glory Lord*, (South Africa: South African Baptist Missionary Society, 1979).

3. Ibid.

4. Andrew Murray quote from "Quotes on Prayer," http://www.onlyinternet.net/lori/quotes_on_prayer.htm (accessed December 22, 2008).

5. Dictionary.com, s.v. "apartheid," http://dictionary.reference.com/browse/apartheid (accessed December 22, 2008).

6. Innocent English.com, http://www.innocentenglish.com/popular-boy-girl-baby-names/baby-girls-name-database-meaning/baby-girls-names1.html (accessed December 22, 2008).

CHAPTER 6
1. Andrew Murray quote found at "Tentmaker Quotes," http://www.tentmaker.org/Quotes/prayerquotes.htm (accessed December 22, 2008).

2. "Transformation" from http://www.transformationsvideo.org/s09.asp (accessed December 22, 2008.

3. Catherine Marshall quote found at "Tentmaker Quotes," http://www.tentmaker.org/Quotes/prayerquotes.htm (accessed December 22, 2008).

CHAPTER 8
1. NationMaster.com, "Langa, South Africa," http://www.nationmaster.com/encyclopedia/Langa,-South-Africa (accessed December 22, 2008).

2. Wikipedia.org, s.v. "ubuntu", http://en.wikipedia.org/wiki/Ubuntu_(philosophy) (accessed December 22, 2008).

CHAPTER 9
1. *Cape Times*, Thursday, March 22, 2001.

2. *Cape Arugus*, Friday, April 6, 2001.

3. *Helderberg Post*, Thursday, April 5, 2001.

Chapter 10

1. John Wesley quote found at "Tentmaker Quotes," http://www.tentmaker. org/Quotes/prayerquotes.htm (accessed December 22, 2008).

Chapter 11

1. Oswald Chambers quote found at "Tentmaker Quotes," http://www.tent-maker.org/Quotes/prayerquotes.htm (accessed December 22, 2008).

2. Brother Lawrence quote found at "Christian Prayer Quotations," http:// www.christian-prayer-quotes.christian-attorney.net/ (accessed December 22, 2008).

Chapter 12

1. Transformation Broadcast quote taken from video footage of the event. 2002.

2. John Climacus quote found at "Tentmaker Quotes," http://www.tent-maker.org/Quotes/prayerquotes.htm (accessed December 22, 2008).

3. Phillips Brooks quote found at Brainyquote.com, http://www.brainyquote. com/quotes/quotes/p/phillipsbr122078.html (accessed December 22, 2008).

Chapter 13

1. Oswald Chambers quote found at "Tentmaker Quotes," http://www.tent-maker.org/Quotes/prayerquotes.htm (accessed December 23, 2008).

Chapter 15

1. James Edwin Orr quote found at Jericho Walls International Prayer Network "Prayer Pointers," http://www.jwipn.com/prayer_pointers. asp?y=2008&m=12&d=15&p=1 (accessed December 23, 2008).

Chapter 16

1. Leonard Ravenhill quote found at "Tentmaker Quotes," http://www.tent-maker.org/Quotes/prayerquotes.htm (accessed December 23, 2008).

Chapter 17

1. Leonard Ravenhill quote found at "Leonard Ravenhill: A Man of God," http://www.scrollpublishing.com/store/ravenhill.html (accessed December 23, 2008).

2. Quote taken from GOD TV live recording of the event in Hong Kong.

Chapter 19

1. http://www.transparency.org/policy_research/surveys_indices/cpi (accessed September 23, 2008).

Business

Pledge
FORM

Unashamedly
Ethical
SOUTH AFRICA

As a business person, professional or employee, committed to transformation, I pledge:

- To be ethical, operating in the highest integrity to produce and deliver quality products and services, including:

  o   Refusal to accept or pay bribes
  o   Paying taxes
  o   Paying reasonable salaries/wages

- To intentionally invest in the betterment of my workforce and their families.
- To actively pursue the transformation of my sphere of influence and expertise in the marketplace.
- To invest generously and sacrificially in the broader community with the focus on eradicating systemic poverty.
- To purposefully connect with other companies, professions and individuals to impact the world.

Signature_____

Signed on the____day of_____,200____in_____.

I hereby agree that my information may be added to the database for use of future communications:

YES ☐   NO ☐

Please complete the following:

Name and Surname: _____

Name of Department: _____

E-mail Address: _____

Telephone Number: _____ Mobile Number: _____

Your Postal Address: _____

transformation

Please fax or e-mail the completed form to the Office:
Phone:+27 21 856 4140 Fax:+27 86 673 9720
E-mail:info@unashamedlyethical.com
Website:http://www.unashamedlyethical.com
PO Box 3856 Somerset West 7129

Your
Business
Logo

Education Pledge FORM

Unashamedly Ethical SOUTH AFRICA

As a Transformation School, Tertiary Institute, individual student or a employed young adult, I pledge:

- To be ethical, operating in the highest integrity and living values that will positively influence society, e.g.:
  - Respecting the authorities placed over us
  - Focusing on the needs of others, rather than achieving success at the expense of others
  - Refusal to accept or pay bribes, or being forced to become involved in any practice that would endanger a safe living environment for all.
- To intentionally invest in the betterment of the people in my sphere of influence and their families.
- To actively pursue the transformation of my sphere of influence.
- To use my resources, time and talents to help eradicate poverty in the broader community.
- To purposefully connect with other young friends on campus or at the work place to impact our community and nation.

Signature_____

Signed on the____day of_____,200____in_____.

I hereby agree that my information may be added to the database for use of future communications:

YES ☐   NO ☐

Please complete the following:

Name and Surname: _____

Name of Department: _____

E-mail Address: _____

Telephone Number: _____ Mobile Number: _____

Your Postal Address: _____

Please fax or e-mail the completed form to the Office:
Phone:+27 21 856 4140 Fax:+27 86 673 9720
E-mail:info@unashamedlyethical.com
Website:http://www.unashamedlyethical.com
PO Box 3856 Somerset West 7129

Your Business Logo

Ministry
Pledge
FORM

Unashamedly
Ethical
SOUTH AFRICA

As a Church/Ministry Leader, committed to transformation, I pledge:

* To equip, commission and release my members to reach the marketplace and pastor the city/region 24/7.

* To diligently pursue the organic unity of the larger Body of Christ to energize the mission of the Church.

* To commit a growing percentage of my resources to kingdom expansion by sacrificially investing beyond the local congregation/ministry to achieve the objective of transformation.

* To expect the Kingdom of God to be tangibly manifested in cities and nations.

Signature_____

Signed on the____day of_____,200____in_____.

I hereby agree that my information may be added to the database for use of future communications:

YES ☐   NO ☐

Please complete the following:

Name and Surname: _____

Name of Department: _____

E-mail Address: _____

Telephone Number: _____   Mobile Number: _____

Your Postal Address: _____

transformation

Please fax or e-mail the completed form to the Office:
Phone:+27 21 856 4140 Fax:+27 86 673 9720
E-mail:info@unashamedlyethical.com
Website:http://www.unashamedlyethical.com
PO Box 3856 Somerset West 7129

Your
Business
Logo

Government
Pledge
FORM

Unashamedly
Ethical
SOUTH AFRICA

As a Public Servant/elected official, committed to Transformation, I pledge:

- To be ethical, operating in the highest integrity to provide efficient, economic and effective public service delivery in an impartial, fair and equitable manner including:
  - refusing to elicit, accept or pay any bribes;
  - disclosing all personal or family financial interests which may affect decision making;
  - negotiating government contracts with utmost integrity;
  - reporting fraud, corruption, nepotism, maladministration and other offences; and
  - ensuring transparency, accountability and fair administrative action by providing the public with timely, accessible and accurate information.
- To actively invest in the betterment of other state employees/elected officials by good human resource management.
- To actively pursue the transformation of my sphere of influence and expertise in the public service.
- To purposefully connect with other public servants/elected officials/individuals and organisations to positively impact the world.

Signature_____

Signed on the____day of_____,200____in_____.

I hereby agree that my information may be added to the database for use of future communications:

YES ☐   NO ☐

Please complete the following:

Name and Surname: _____

Name of Department: _____

E-mail Address: _____

Telephone Number: _____ Mobile Number: _____

Your Postal Address: _____

transformation

Please fax or e-mail the completed form to the Office:
Phone:+27 21 856 4140 Fax:+27 86 673 9720
E-mail:info@unashamedlyethical.com
Website:http://www.unashamedlyethical.com
PO Box 3856 Somerset West 7129

Your
Business
Logo